George Fetherling
and His Work

ISBN 0-9738645-1-6

Library and Archives Canada Cataloguing in Publication

George Fetherling and his work / Linda Rogers, editor.
Includes interviews and previously unpublished
material by George Fetherling.
Includes bibliographical references.

1. Fetherling, George, 1949- —Criticism and interpretation.
I. Rogers, Linda, 1944-
II. Fetherling, George, 1949-
PS8561.E834Z65 2005   C818'.5409   C2005-904871-9

Printed and bound in Canada
Design by Keith Daniel
Cover photograph ©1996 by Evan Dion, used by permission
Title page image ©2005 George Fetherling

Tightrope Books
17 Greyton Crescent
Toronto, Ontario M6E 2G1
www.tightropebooks.com

In Kate – a strange little book –
something for your cabinet of
curiosities.

George

George Fetherling

AND HIS WORK

September 2005

Edited by Linda Rogers

TIGHTROPE BOOKS
Toronto • Detroit

Contents

The Witness, an Introduction

Linda Rogers[†]

George Fetherling is what Robin Skelton used to call a "scribbler": someone such as himself whose compulsive writing is faster than sound. Sound is a problem. Fetherling, the poet/novelist/artist/ cultural journalist who has mastered the silent word, switching genres with a click of his many-coloured pen, was born with a speech handicap. He has, in the jargon of the differently abled, compensated, the way stutterers are known to sing or recite poetry fluently even though plain speech is difficult. In book after book of articulate prose and poetry, Fetherling (the last name is an anglicized spelling of an old Dutch word for *scribe* or *scrivener*) sings like a bird with a thorn in its chest. Like children born with learning disabilities who often develop prodigious oral and artistic skills, he proves the adaptability of human beings.

In *Travels by Night: A Memoir of the Sixties*, Fetherling describes the genesis of his ability to change shapes so adroitly, growing up in a dysfunctional family whose matrix was secrecy. His father was George Singer Fetherling whom many called Joe but the writer refers to as Singer in his book-length memorial poem, *Singer, An Elegy*. He himself is Douglas George Fetherling on his Canadian passport and for years wrote as Douglas. In 2000 when he reached the age his father was at his death, he reverently switched to George. Changes of name, changes of mood and changes of personality were the matrix that formed his romantic consciousness.

Fetherling survived a childhood in which his parents, divided by class, had their expectations crushed in the repressive postwar

---

† Linda Rogers is a poet, novelist, editor and children's writer. Her most recent books include the novel *Friday Water* (2003).

industrial society. At the very best, his early life can be said to have prepared him for the generational gulf that set up the political dialectic of the sixties, when wartime and postwar babies had grown to demand the legislation of peace and civil rights from their conflicted elders. Perhaps it was through growing up in a familial war zone that he was able to reject the culture's shameful political legacy of bullying intolerance, leaving it behind him at an early age and with such finality.

Like such other prodigious readers as Al Purdy, George Woodcock and Susan Musgrave, Fetherling is an autodidact, with a hunger for knowledge that demands a curriculum far more rigorous than that of any university. His teachers have been the great scientists, historians, poets and philosophers. Going directly to the sources, he has learned to think for himself. Canada, where alpha males are the subject of satire, is the right environment for someone who admires the Chinese poet Li Po, knew the poet–activist Allen Ginsberg and wrote a life of George Woodcock that articulates the potential for secular redemption. Finding a state of grace is no easy matter in a world controlled by the rhetoric of Wall Street and Texas.

When asked about seminal influences, most people mention childhood books, perhaps *Narnia* or *A Child's Garden of Verses*. Fetherling is different, and speaks instead of an era in Toronto when Canada, after a self-conscious artistic infancy, finally entered its cultural heyday. He already knew that social responsibility was the means to personal and cultural redemption. Before the western world rode the doctrine of selfishness to the present, there was, in the words of *Camelot*, a brief shining moment when it looked as though pragmatic idealism could write a new world order based on peace and love. Fetherling was one of its anonymous architects, thinking to ignite the new culture with the ideals of cautious optimism. Those were the days when a new group of writers became the voice of the land, challenging the status quo without abandoning the gospel of compassion. Living in the basement of

Dave Godfrey's House of Anansi, Fetherling witnessed the rise of Canadian writers like Margaret Atwood, Dennis Lee, Gwendolyn MacEwen and Michael Ondaatje as oracles of our time who did much to make Canadian literature an international force. "I was there, the one outside the frame when the photos were cropped," he says modestly.

And yet it is true that he has never become a household name. Although the name appeared regularly on the literary pages of major newspapers and magazines, he remained a witness, for reasons that have to do with charisma, timing and integrity. He writes with intelligence and clarity, and his voice is distinct, yet he is still a witness, a role no doubt established in the theatre of his early life when he made the decision to render himself invisible. Now invisibility is second nature, in spite of an impressive canon of work that runs to dozens of books including not only poetry and fiction but criticism and travel narrative and such engaging oddities as *The Book of Assassins*, a kind of cultural encyclopedia of how political assassination has created different assumptions in different cultures at different times in history.

In his *Selected Poems* appears this line: "The child who grows up shall remember." Memory is the precursor to caution. In another poem, he writes that the "inability to trust another person / is nature's defence against intrigue." In the world of artists, many of whom have the instincts of barracudas, diplomacy is essential to survival, and sometimes George, like the eunuchs of the Imperial court, wears silk slippers. Changing how he styles himself, he has dodged and weaved, arguing with himself in the cultural commentary he has staked out as his intellectual territory.

Wise people say that human beings need something to look forward to. Thus the phenomenon of the dying who hang on until a significant moment is achieved: a birthday, Christmas, the birth of a child. In Fetherling's terms, looking forward would mean the next journey, the next book. He keeps moving, "travelling by night" even in the daytime, wearing his various costumes and aliases, blending into the landscape, as he did, for instance, in Burma, where writers are anathema and he posed as a gemologist seeking the perfect ruby. When he confronts a barrier, he approaches it the way he first tackled language, looking for the back door, a way in. Although never a parent, he has a rapport with students and says he enjoys teaching as an adjunct to the literary life. He has been a writer-in-residence several times, at institutions big and small, taking advantage of pedagogical opportunities that have eluded him otherwise because of his speech impediment. Fetherling has the experience, information and passion essential to an outstanding performer or teacher, but those doors have remained closed to him, sometimes in spite of the endorsement of celebrities he has helped to create. In giving me a piece of advice about how to deal with other people's cruelty, he taught me that wounds can be doors to self-understanding. Like all his lessons, it was leavened with irony. "I don't always agree with the Dalai Lama," he said with a laugh, "but he's right about that." The *that* was that we should forgive—and travel light.

"I have been fortunate in my friendships," Fetherling says. "I use my limited gifts to the best of my ability." I have heard accompanists describe themselves as sound enhancers, whose professional pride rests in making others sound better. Perhaps that is enough to ask of a man whose voice was compromised from the beginning. It is enough to sing in the choir if the choir is stronger because he is there. If he can improve the human condition, word by word, then he is satisfied. The hard part is deciding how to establish working priorities. Visual art is also important to Fetherling, whose craft bears the imprint of a close observer of the phenomenal world. Those observations, combined with a keen intellectual awareness of the patterns in nature and human nature, are the hallmarks of his writing.

Wanting to understand when it is he believes fiction becomes non-fiction and non-fiction becomes fiction, I asked if the female acquaintances featured in two of his travel narratives, *Running Away to Sea* and *Three Pagodas Pass*, are in fact only a literary device. My suspicions were raised by the ones who turn up in the travel books of Pico Iyer to embody the character of every country he visits. In Iyer's case, the device becomes repetitious (and in his fiction it is so artificial that it actually undermines the state of suspended disbelief he requests of the reader). With Fetherling, the female antagonists serve to heighten the tension of the journey, exacerbating whatever deprivations or discomforts already exist in the landscape or providing contrast to the pilgrim's naïve appreciation of a fresh cultural milieu. Fetherling insists these women are real, but I have to wonder if they are nevertheless aspects of the irrational voice in his head that follows wherever he goes, spouting non-sequiturs, compelling his careful scholarly quest to comprehend the world on his own terms. Perhaps by moving the focus of drama away from himself, he is reinforcing a dispassionate point of view, "his face like that of an archaeologist / afraid of what he will discover," to quote another of his poems.

George Fetherling, trickster, shape and name changer, has been an enigma on my bookshelves, as he has been on those of every contributor to this collection. Their considerations of various aspects of this blackbird that sings with grace (in spite or because of the pebbles in his mouth) make an interesting whole. The portrait they paint is measured in brushstrokes and wing beats—a poem here, a review there, a novel beyond. All the books—fiction, poetry and non-fiction alike—are about journeys of the geographical, sexual and philosophical kinds. In contrast to George Elliott Clarke, who sees Fetherling's poetry as deriving from the settled Red Tory tradition rather like that from which he himself sprang in Nova Scotia, W.H. New ventures inside the outsider by using poems as signposts on the borderland between self and other. He writes with insight and clarity of how, in poetry fashioned with a painter's eye and with the heightened awareness of an autodidact, Fetherling teaches us how to cross mined urban landscapes to past and future realities. Eric Marks, a young poet and reviewer, does something similar with regard to Fetherling's prose.

Most revealing of Fetherling the interdisciplinary man-of-letters is John Clement Ball's interview, in which Fetherling gives storm warnings about how the arts can be deadened by complacency as easily as social freedom or political and economic autonomy can. It is a wide-ranging discussion about the state of publishing, reviewing and the system of grants and awards built by committee and consensus and now threatened by its own virtues. The interview gives a true sample of Fetherling's public voice and works well with Brian Busby's description of Fetherling's private voice, as heard in thousands of pages of unpublished journals. With somewhat the same purpose, Jennifer Toews of the Thomas Fisher Rare Book Library at the University of Toronto, where Fetherling's papers are held, describes her delightful correspondence with this travelling magician who keeps an eye on the literary terrain, hunting down errata.

John Burns describes another type of encounter. He recounts how a fruitful professional relationship began at Vancouver's legendary Sylvia Hotel (better known as a place where writers meet in the bar and bed one another upstairs). The framework for their dialogue is mutual respect: Fetherling is always respectful of his fellow writers and hopes that they will respond in kind. Rhonda Batchelor writes of Fetherling's relationship with her late husband Charles Lillard, another writer with a great thirst for life and appetite for wisdom.

Writers are often described as outsiders, and Fetherling is the paradigm: a generalist in the age of specialization who, when driven to stand outside, has made the world his house, throwing open its many rooms to discourse. In a profession that invites self-absorption, Fetherling writes his own transparencies, the story of a larger world that is all the better for his presence.

Travels in the Cosmopolitan World of George Fetherling

Eric Marks[†]

The contrarian journalist Charles Fort once summed up his working method with the observation, "One measures a circle, beginning anywhere." A haphazard approach, perhaps, but it has its uses—particularly when pondering the corpus of a writer as richly prolific as George Fetherling. His dozens of published volumes include lyric and long poetry, fiction, memoir, social history, biography, journalism, travel literature and collections of cultural criticism that range in focus from newspapers to cinema, and from the visual arts to songwriting. He has received the most acclaim as a poet, and the widest audience as a journalist. The only label that comes close to encompassing the breadth of his accomplishments is man-of-letters.

The writers we think of as men and women of letters were people of ideas first, who marked out intellectual territories that circumscribed their diverse endeavours. Readers of Fetherling's various books will find many of them united by certain ideas. Begin reading wherever you will; you will eventually turn upon these paths.

[†] Eric Marks was a Rhodes Scholar at Oxford and is now a poet, reviewer and editor in his native Saint John, New Brunswick.

Rather than attempt an exhaustive survey of Fetherling's prose, I propose to trace a couple of the major ideas that thread through his works, culminating in his recent novel, *Jericho*. The following ought to be taken as something of an impressionistic sketch, not unlike Fetherling's portraits of Canadian authors. The goal is to convey some sense of the literary terrain he inhabits, and his character as a writer—if only the glint in his eye and the jut of his bones.

2

An important element in Fetherling's writing is the value he places on the man-of-letters. In projects that range from his biography of George Woodcock to his memoirs and brief reminiscences of Gwendolyn MacEwen and Margaret Atwood, he pays tribute to those whose practice fits this pattern. A student of Fetherling would be remiss not to take note of this, as it provides some justification for considering his work as an oeuvre.

In a 1992 interview with Katie Sykes published in *Queen's Quarterly* and collected in *Jive Talk: George Fetherling in Interviews and Documents*, he articulates his understanding of the label:

> People use the term as an accolade, as though it were a grade of writer or a rank. In fact, it's a type of writer, someone who is both a creative writer and a critical writer, a jack of all trades who, as [George] Woodcock says, is able to turn his or her hand to whatever needs doing at the moment. It means having a lot of tools to express the ideas that you work out for yourself over the years. Is not Margaret Atwood a woman of letters in that sense? Was not Virginia Woolf? If what she wanted to say at a particular time was best said in a lecture, in an essay, or in a piece of fiction, the appropriate form presented itself (*Jive Talk*, 29).

In Fetherling's works, the man-of-letters is closely linked with the autodidact. As a young man whose stutter and social circumstances prevented success in the classroom, Fetherling writes, "The search for books pushed me to search out people who might at least have read ones I couldn't find [....] In this way I located individuals with some taste for learning which they had been forced to paint over if they were to find even a modest place in the oppressive ignorance of darkest America" (*Travels by Night*, 44). Among those so located were "aged anarcho-syndicalists and other survivors of the old radical culture," including a man who had worked as a reader in a cigar factory, intoning Goethe and Schiller and Stendhal to a roomful of immigrant men as they rolled stogies, and "Mary Tominack, who had the greatest beneficial influence on me of anyone." Fetherling portrays this self-educated activist as nondescript, but formidable:

> She was a presence or a force in groups as far apart as the Congress of Racial Equality and the Sexual Freedom League; the friend, comforter and prodder of agitators, martyrs, refugees, renegades, subversives, outlaws, cranks, dietary reformers and, of course, folk singers [...] She naturally didn't own any cats but looked after a dozen or so. When the cats' rightful masters and mistresses came to retrieve them, she converted their children to vegetarianism and gave them free piano lessons. She was wonderful" (*Travels*, 46-7).

Of the other autodidacts encountered in Fetherling's work, the one accorded most prominence is George Woodcock, the British-born anarchist philosopher who, like Fetherling, chose to live in Canada. Woodcock, Fetherling notes, "always used to say that he wrote books on particular topics—on Tibet or the Greeks or Aldous Huxley or whatever—in order to learn more about those topics; that writing the books was in a way just incidental to the process of acquiring the knowledge," to which the writer adds, "I'm a bit like that, I guess" (*Jive Talk*, 65).

In characterizing his early ambitions, Fetherling suggests he may have had such examples in mind when he determined to take up journalism. He reflects, "I thought of myself as a writer. I was gradually pulling together a thick manuscript of poems [....] But I wanted to try every type of writing, not only poetry, so as to be led naturally to whatever form seemed appropriate to the immediate purpose" (*Travels*, 69).

This is a practical consideration. If one accepts "the sad truth that a writer's most powerful place in society is as no writer at all, but as a sort of wholesaler of opinions, esoterica and general ideas" (*Jive Talk*, 27), then the most successful writers are those who can employ language with the greatest dexterity, suiting form to purpose as seamlessly as possible.

Knowing the value he places on this approach to literature, readers may wish to consider Fetherling's texts as utterances in a sustained conversation, as well as discrete works of literature, and to view his own utterances as part of that discourse.

3

Fetherling has acknowledged that "the nature of America vis-à-vis Canada, and its pernicious influence" is an underlying theme in much of his writing (*Jive Talk*, 11–2). But Fetherling's treatment of this subject has more nuance to it than some have been willing to concede. The dichotomy he establishes represents a long-standing struggle between opposing qualities in the human spirit: the will to dominate set against the will to be free, selfishness and greed set against co-operation and liberality, the provincial or nativist outlook set against the cosmopolitan. The political border between "America" and "Canada" is less important than the gulf between the values they embody, a difference Fetherling portrays as the essential distinction between the imperial and post-colonial temperaments.

This dichotomy is developed in the starkest terms in *Travels by Night*. Fetherling casts his story as that of a precocious child whose coming-to-consciousness is shaped by his divided family, which he comes to see as a microcosm of America's polarization by McCarthyism and the Vietnam War. He portrays his decision to seek Canadian citizenship as a clear choice of political and cultural values opposed to the values he sees at work in America: "The abiding [Canadian] tradition of anti-Americanism, always present deep down in the lay public if not always pursued by cowardly governments, was one I found especially attractive" (*Travels*, 95).

While *Travels by Night* corresponds to the conventions of memoir, it is also a sustained argument for liberal values and intentional communities, an argument Fetherling sets in motion by making personal circumstances seem profoundly political. Elsewhere, Fetherling has stated that "in terms of cultural values, the Americans on the one hand and the British world on the other are separate and distinct" (*Jive Talk*, 25). It's a distinction he emphasizes in describing the dynamic of his parents' household.

His father is depicted as a gentle, loving figure, a man at once urbane and urban—upper middle class in background, at ease in the modern city, well read, polite, witty, artistic. Prevented from going to university by the financial constraints of the Great Depression, he turns to work as a machinist and marries below his social station. Fetherling characterizes his father's cultural values as British: "He had, I feel, an essentially English character, so rare in an American. He must have sensed that, without quite realizing what it was that made him so out of place" (*Travels*, 7). This comes to provide an explanation for his father's isolation, not simply in American public life, but in their Wheeling, West Virginia, home.

The writer's mother is introduced as his father's antithesis. She is described in a "revealing" snapshot as "a young girl in flapper clothes standing in a patch of mud, trying to look urbane and urban, pursing her lips and feigning a kind of sophisticated disinterest [....] From her earliest period of consciousness, my mother disliked her life and surroundings but lacked any means of improving or changing them, was bound to them, in fact, by the twists and turns of her personality" (*Travels*, 12). Her behaviour is, by turns, selfish, envious, hateful, spitefully ignorant and psychotic, though she is redeemed somewhat by the writer's awareness that she, like his father, has been wounded deeply by circumstances that thwarted her ambitions: "It must have been a special kind of torture for her to be a teenager in the Roaring Twenties, yearning to be part of Flaming Youth but knowing that, though the popular culture found its way even to the hills behind Martins Ferry, there was no possibility that she could be a part of what it represented" (*Travels*, 12–3). After her death, the author discovers "she had been born in Martins Ferry but had chosen Canton [Ohio] because it sounded to her so much more cosmopolitan. It was at that time I learned she wasn't a high school graduate" (*Travels*, 10).

The union between a couple so at odds cannot be anything but a catastrophe, and so it proves to be: "She seemed to promise the anonymity he was seeking, the total workaday world that would offer no reminders of what he was because it brooked no comparison with what he might have been. From her point of view, he was her ticket to the bright lights. Their expectations contradicted each other. The resulting disaster went on for more than twenty-five years" (*Travels*, 13).

But what another writer might have explored as a purely personal tragedy, or a clash of social expectations, Fetherling elevates to an example of conflicting values in the larger world. He makes a point of recording that Senator Joe McCarthy delivered his speech denouncing "205 communists" in the State Department in Wheeling, though Fetherling was only one year old when this occurred. Indeed, the writer depicts his hometown as the epicentre and birthplace of McCarthyism, a place so culturally primed for nativist aggression and oppression that a year earlier a gum wrapper from a series saluting the nations of the world caused a furor, because it "featured the Soviet flag and the hated name Moscow [....] [T]his was held to be a trick for propagating godless communism among impressionable Wheelingites. Such was the political atmosphere in which I was growing up" (*Travels*, 42).

The family household and the city thus became a miniature proving ground for the political traditions beginning to diverge in the 1950s and 1960s, worldviews that Fetherling depicts as mutually exclusive. With the advent of the Vietnam War, the dividing line was drawn: "I did know in so many words what the larger difficulty appeared to be. The problem was not the war, the problem was America" (*Travels*, 93). The remedy he chose was to seek refuge elsewhere, in a community of different values. With the encouragement of intellectuals whose cosmopolitan outlook echoed his father's, Fetherling turned to Canada:

> Since the day Mary Tominack first put the notion of Canada in my head, I had been subscribing to Canadian periodicals and through [my girlfriend] Jasmine's example monitoring the CBC. In time I got to the point of maintaining a correspondence with a few Canadian writers. [....] I deepened my commitment to learning Canadian politics, economics, culture—the works [....] I was careful not to let my own enthusiasms shape my curriculum. For the only time in my life, I was a serious pupil in addition to being a good student (*Travels*, 95).

Fetherling's embrace of Canada is not a matter of exchanging nationalisms; on the contrary, he suggests nationalism is part of the problem in America:

> Emerson said that being an American was not a national-

ity as such but a moral condition. He was close. It is an immoral condition. [....] No one was contending that one government was necessarily better than another in its potential for good or disposition towards evil (by this time I'd discovered George Woodcock). Some are simply worse, more vicious, more stupid, wholly owned subsidiaries of the devil, because they mirror the culture, in the broadest sense, that supports them. Yet, perversely and triumphantly, it's only in their culture that one society sometimes expresses qualities that transcend their governments and their businessmen and so help compensate for them (*Travels*, 101).

In America's foreign and domestic policies, Fetherling finds an analogue for the envious, domineering and destructive behaviour of his mother:

In 1966, I thought that Americans were the salt of the earth: and so wherever they walked, nothing would ever grow again. What was most astounding was their hard shell of ignorance that seemed to preclude any acknowledgement of guilt. And they had so much to be guilty for. The business of America, Calvin Coolidge's remark to the contrary, was not just business, it was everybody else's business, an attitude that inevitably led to violence. (*Travels*, 99–100).

It is not just the social environment of America he is fleeing, nor its political institutions, but the bankruptcy of the values underlying them, a bankruptcy mirrored in his family's dissolution: "There was no moral commitment because there was no civilization worth the name, and no civilization because there was no education, no humaneness, no sense of the necessity of ongoing improvement, except in a few brave and isolated people, saintly really, whose lives showed what culture really was" (*Travels*, 101).

The cosmopolitan world view Fetherling identifies with these neglected values, with his father and with Canada, has much in common with the qualities he celebrates in men- and women-of-letters. For what is cosmopolitanism but a catholicity of outlook and a fluency in ideas?

4

Travels by Night represents Fetherling's most direct attack on the inhumane values he identifies with America, but as a social historian, he has taken up similar analyses in different form. In particular, *The Gold Crusades: A Social History of Gold Rushes, 1849–1929* (1988, revised 1997) examines how sharply America and other English-speaking nations have diverged from their common British heritage.

In this study of "the Argonauts" who pursued the chimera of easy wealth from California to Nevada, Australia, South Africa and the Klondike, Fetherling argues, "A true gold rush is predicated on freedom of movement coupled with a belief in people's ability to better themselves. That is to say, gold rushes were an outgrowth of British liberalism, related to both free trade and home rule" (*Gold Crusades*, 5). From this vantage point, "The subtext of the gold rushes—and a pretty obvious one it is—was the struggle between order and chaos, between authority and lawlessness, between British and American ideas of society" (*Gold Crusades*, 7). In the worst cases, "gold rushes came to mean overreaching, greed, fraud, violence—in any case, no cooperative commonwealth"—a pattern Fetherling attributes to the fact "the first gold rush took place on American soil" (*Gold Crusades*, 5).

The most trenchant example of how these two political traditions divide, Fetherling suggests, is "the one crystallized by Pierre Berton: how order and good government prevailed in Dawson, on the Yukon side of the Canada-US boundary, while violence and corruption were the hallmarks of Skagway, on the Alaskan side" (*Gold Crusades*, 8).

Fetherling's achievement in this book—a far more subversive one than *Travels by Night*—is to stand the American view of the gold rush on its head, by placing the phenomenon in an international context that reveals the American example to have been an anomaly, rather than the norm. In effect, he reclaims the history of the gold rushes in support of a rival cultural tradition— the liberal heritage of the Commonwealth—arguing that "viewing Canada's or Australia's gold rush as part of a cumulative worldwide development is not inconsistent with the best instincts of Canadian or Australian nationalism. On the contrary, to do so is to seek in the British imperial heritage a rival form of individual expression that is separate from Americanism and untainted by it" (*Gold Crusades*, 8).

5

This search for "rival forms of individual expression" may be seen in Fetherling's travel writing as well, though not all of the cultures he explores honour human values. And not all of the oppressive values he encounters stem from the influence of America.

Like the speaker in his poem "Our Man in Utopia" whose calm observations belie the ominous changes taking place in the society he is reporting on, Fetherling bears witness to the repression of humanist values by governments. Where a tourist might be content to look for cultural differences, he becomes an inquirer, probing for cultural values. This political interest stands out strongly in *Three Pagodas Pass: A Roundabout Journey to Burma* (2002), in which he attempts to take the cultural pulse of one of the world's most totalitarian regimes.

Fetherling's interest in Southeast Asia derives from "what the Vietnamese call 'the American War'" but his interest in Burma is more specific:

[T]he longest ongoing insurgency in the world is taking place there. It's now in its fifty-first year, with the ethnic minorities against the evil junta who control the government, who combine all the worst features of communism and capitalism, who are communists in that old Stalinist/North Korean kind of way but are also by far the dominant figures in the world's heroin trade [....] As a character says in John Boorman's movie *Beyond Rangoon*, "In Burma, everything is illegal" (*Jive Talk*, 66).

Fetherling's goal is not merely to see Rangoon, which he does, but to visit the Burmese hinterland. He attempts to do so at Three Pagodas Pass, a wild spot on the Thai-Burmese border with a reputation for anarchy. "Because it had always been a kind of free-market no-man's-land, the Pass was the obvious place for me to test the current level of tolerance, though I wasn't sure how I was going to be greeted" (*Three Pagodas*, 103). What he finds is a sad flea market of Burmese vendors on the Thai side, selling "notorious furniture that is made before the wood has been properly dried and so is bound to crack and split," "old military fatigues," helmets and knives. "All of this was in addition to the wood carvings, fake Rolexes, glass gemstones, cigarette lighters, and general pieces of junk that are the trade goods of the modern world. At least no one at Three Pagodas Pass sold T-shirts printed with THREE PAGODAS PASS, for this is still thankfully more of a black market than a souvenir stand. In some places history still obtains" (*Three Pagodas*, 104).

The nadir of this deflating experience, though, is the moment when he finds himself "transfixed" by the sight of a battered M-16 rifle in the arms of a Burmese soldier. Reflecting that the American assault rifle and its Soviet counterpart were first brought to the region during the colonial wars of the 1960s, he observes:

Here we were more than a full generation later and the world was divided by brand loyalty as well as by every sort of racial, ethnic, religious, and political difference. Both the American M-16 and the Russian Kalashnikov designs were now being knocked off by any number of nations with no respect for intellectual property. Both weapons had undergone improvements as they became cheaper and more ubiquitous [....] Some always would choose the rip-off of the American technology, while others inevitably would pick up the AK-47 or one of its younger siblings, two of whose banana clips can be joined together with duct tape for twice its rival's load. Like PC and Mac users, or Coke and Pepsi drinkers, never the twain shall meet. One day there will be a war between people separated by nothing more than such preferences in the tools of war (*Three Pagodas*, 105).

What Fetherling discovers on the Thai–Burmese border is the erasure of culture itself, along with the erasure of liberty, carried out by the adherents of two different ideological systems, each perverted to serve the same narrow, dehumanizing agenda: greed and the urge to control. The Burma he depicts in *Three Pagodas Pass* is the endpoint of the inhumane values he rails against in *Travels by Night*—the geopolitical embodiment of George Orwell's *Nineteen Eighty-Four*, or of the unnamed state capital described in "Our Man in Utopia." One in three citizens is a government informer. Everything is forbidden. And the economy is "in a shambles [....] Burma's main exportable manufactured goods are barbed wire and methamphetamines. And the barbed wire is only what's surplus to the domestic market, which uses the stuff by the kilometre to imprison dissenters, democrats, and ethnic minorities" (*Three Pagodas*, 152).

Part of the equation he sketches seems clear: imperialism and commerce, accelerated by technology, equals globalization. But does globalization necessarily equal the death of humanist values?

6

Fetherling addresses that question imaginatively in his novel *Jericho* (2005), which attends to two related concerns: "the loss of the modernist city" and "how we continue humanism in a post-urban or post-downtown age" (*Jive Talk*, 22–23).

Fetherling has expressed fascination with the notion that "there was a Byzantium that slipped out of our grasp"—a higher level of civilization, in service to human values, that America turned away from. This "modernist notion of the American city of skyscrapers, the beneficial perpetual motion machine, was really the glory of the New World" (*Jive Talk*, 22).

Its potential was destroyed, in Fetherling's analysis, by the suburbs and superhighways created in response to fears of racial integration and nuclear annihilation. As such, "It was killed out of stupidity; it was killed by greed" and by "white racism" (*Jive Talk*, 23). The consequences for urban life have been dire: the abandonment of cities to poverty and brutality, fast approaching the conditions described in *Three Pagodas Pass*. His prognosis, in 1992, was gloomy: "I'm sure in time the centre of human gravity will be driven entirely out into the suburbs. The last of the city will be given over to people who sell cheap knockoffs of cheap originals" (ibid).

If the future for America "is not pleasant," Fetherling implies Canada may be able to avoid this fate. While Canadian cities have followed a similar pattern, there is one significant difference: the multiculturalism that has shaped Canadian development in recent decades.

Fetherling describes this as a legacy of the Commonwealth, arguing that the "kind of multiculturalism that we have in Canada, that they have in Australia, and in other places, is a British invention. The British opened up London in 1945 to people who were dislocated by the turmoil in the late war and the break-up of the empire. That was how London ceased to be the city that it had been and became the city that it is today. Our multiculturalism is, in a sense, the result of that" (*Jive Talk*, 26).

In *Jericho*, which he has characterized as "a downtown fable," Fetherling contrasts one vision of the future against the other. The plot of the novel is easily summarized: Bishop, an aging hippie, robs a video store and flees Vancouver's Downtown Eastside for the Interior, accompanied by Beth, a relative innocent from rural Alberta, and Theresa, a neurotic social worker who has attached herself to Beth. The three fugitives hide out at Jericho, a kind of ready-made ghost town, until they are discovered; Bishop is captured and imprisoned, and the two women rebuild their lives. *Jericho* plays with and against conventions of the crime novel, the road novel, the pastoral novel and the lost-in-the-wilderness novel without giving in to any of our expectations. And, further confounding expectations, it features three narrators, each speaking in the first person, each given equal weight and authority by the author.

This multiplicity is the key to unlocking *Jericho*'s identity: by intercutting three equally weighted narrative voices and playing with the conventions of many genres, Fetherling creates a towering Babel of a novel. It's a narrative strategy well suited to *Jericho*'s subtext, which involves competing visions of the urban and different strategies for conveying the values of the past into the future.

Bishop poses as a champion of the old modernist conception of the city, though he doesn't quite know what he is championing. An autodidact but not an intellectual, he is intoxicated by the power of an idea he has not wholly understood. He believes he can "plant the seed" of a new urbanism in the wilderness by artificially giving life to his collection of tumbledown buildings (*Jericho*, 178). The weakness in his ideas can be seen in his understanding of the biblical Jericho and his idea of urban civilization, or "Civ":

> Something got started there that's only begun to die in our lifetime, or in my lifetime anyway [....] It got warm inside

a city with walls like that and a new kind of life form developed, like something in a glass dish in a lab. I mean the downtown life form. People that made everything they needed or had it brought to them, right. I'm talking about the invention of room service. They weren't farmers who lived back of nowhere and worried about if they had enough manure. They weren't nomads either—what we'd call commuters. Eventually they even stopped being straight city folks, Citizens. They lived by their wits, doing a little of this and a little of that (*Jericho*, 168-69).

Bishop's contempt for "Citizens"—urban squares he equates with "the suckers, the rubes, the farmers"—reveals that the city he pines for is the crime-ridden and corrupt metropolis that the modern city became: a place where the inhabitants are divided into predators and victims (*Jericho*, 170). His dream city is modelled on the "Snaketown" of his childhood, which he speaks of with nostalgia as "one of those places where sometimes everybody seemed to be named Smith" (*Jericho*, 34). What Bishop doesn't seem to realize is that Snaketown is the antecedent of the more brutalized Downtown Eastside he has fled. The urban vision Bishop tries to sell is a cheap knockoff of a cheap original. Twice removed from the modernist ideal, it is devoid of the humanist values that inspired the great cities in the first place. It substitutes street smarts for cosmopolitanism.

Just how low Bishop is aiming can be glimpsed in the ease with which he adapts to life in the penitentiary—and how closely prison society resembles the "Civilization" he's longed for:

There aren't any Citizens in this place but there's definitely a sort of Civ. It's Civ based on respect and fear, the way it should be, and worship of what is or isn't going to happen next. It's like living in a hotel except that nobody does anything for you, only to you: a very bad hotel. But it's also like

being in one of your better hotels: sex and drugs on room
service. (*Jericho* 248).

There is a lot of Jack Kerouac about him, a lot of Neal Cassady. As
one of the other characters observes, "it did explain a lot when
you figure that he was growing up in the sixties" (*Jericho*, 209). But
Bishop is not entirely deluded; he understands that the abandonment of the urban core to gangs and drugs and white flight to the
suburbs are negative developments. It's evident in the comfort he
takes from being imprisoned in "a city shut off by a moat of suburbs from all the other suburbs that lie beyond [...] protecting us
from places even worse. Bet you thought there weren't any places
worse. Don't be naïve" (*Jericho*, 250).

Fortunately, there is another urban vision in *Jericho*, one that
seems to hold more promise. It's revealed mostly through the
narrative of Beth, the young woman from rural Alberta. In many
ways, she is Bishop's antithesis. Bishop chooses self-reliance and
trusts in his own knowledge, even when he doesn't know what he
is doing; Beth seeks consensus, leads by example and tends to the
well-being of others. In the woods, it is Beth who looks after Bishop:
lighting fires, purifying water and performing other practical tasks
he proves incapable of (*Jericho*, 133). And when Jericho burns, it
is Beth who ensures she and Theresa will survive until the police
arrive (*Jericho*, 204-06).

Although she is unworldly and new to Vancouver, Beth exhibits
a more cosmopolitan outlook than streetwise Bishop. She accepts
the city and all those she meets, and after moments of fleeting shock,
fear or puzzlement, she quickly comes to terms with new situations.
She is "an optimist" and learns to hold her tongue rather than speak
judgmentally. In the course of her narrative, which covers many
years, Beth forgives her deadbeat father, establishes a career in the
funeral industry, where her compassion is an asset, and becomes "a

long-time Vancouverite" who loves her neighbourhood "with its old houses and run-down businesses" (*Jericho*, 163).

Beth—short for Bethany, which she discovers is "where Lazarus was from, him and his two sisters"—offers the city its best chance of revival (*Jericho*, 210). Her values are humane, and she is free of the second-hand ideology that blinds Bishop. She, too, turns out to be a grandchild of Snaketown, but unlike Bishop, she has a future. He realizes this in prison:

> She's the straightest person I've ever met, in the good sense of the term—and until I met her I didn't know there was a good sense. Don't get me wrong. She's no Citizen. She doesn't see the world as a straight or bent proposition, but she has her own set of codes you might say. My biggest mistake wasn't Jericho, it was maybe not having good communication with her when I could have (*Jericho*, 221).

Through Beth's narrative, Fetherling addresses the changes taking place in "the culture"—cities giving way to suburbs, cities and suburbs becoming more racially mixed due to immigration, the old religious traditions and polarities giving way to new beliefs and customs as the social landscape changes. The funeral home industry in which Beth works is a metaphor for the nation, "tied up in a lot of tradition and [having] to change pretty quickly or else" (*Jericho*, 254). And while the changes wrought by global commerce are part of the picture, in the form of "the Chain" that is buying up funeral homes, the cultural levelling effect of globalism is not presented as the death knell for Beth's humanism, but as a series of daily challenges she overcomes with courage and compassion.

The implication is that the details of our cultural practice matter less than the values we choose to express in our lives and our communities. Beth's compassion and egalitarianism—the "codes"

Bishop comes to admire—have equipped her to survive, and to infuse new life into her changing community.

Beth is given the novel's last words. The anecdote she tells—about washing the hair of a woman's corpse and "saying the sorts of things I'd say to somebody who'd come into the salon when I was young and had hardly ever been outside Alberta"—marks her as one of those "brave and isolated people, saintly really" whom Fetherling praises in *Travels by Night*, "whose lives showed what culture really was." Beth says of her work in the prep room of the funeral parlour:

> I never feel completely alone when I'm down there, for you're always aware that there's another human being there with you, a real man or woman [....] I was doing her hair, like I say, and I heard these words come out of my mouth: "Why can't we talk to the living the way you and I are doing now?" (*Jericho*, 259)

Why indeed?

The Agent[†]

GEORGE FETHERLING

What do you want for your birthday? I asked.

A divorce, she said.

Having half my life cut away made the remaining part more complicated. I was living in a vacant house (it was vacant even when I was there) with important papers all over the floor: manuscripts still not read, contracts yet to be negotiated. Finally I got myself together to go to Office Depot and buy five very cheap plastic briefcases, all bright yellow. I stencilled a different keyword on each one—DIVORCE, WORK etc. One said just T (for THERAPY). I kept them all in a neat row by the door. I thought this was the perfect system but of course it got screwed up. I was having a meeting with the most important publisher in town. I reached down under the boardroom table for my presentation and saw the word DIVORCE two inches high. Later, in the underground garage, I actually cried a little bit. Then I got angry with myself for not colour-coding the fucking things.

It got to the point where I was seeing two different shrinks because I couldn't trust a single individual with everything that was

[†] An excerpt from *Tales of Two Cities* (2006).

going on. After each session, I would have to hurry to the Gents and scribble down notes on what I'd said, so I wouldn't get confused and pick up the story I'd been telling Doctor A when I was having a session with Doctor B. Therapy was actually making me schizoid, I thought. Eventually I revised my system. Two briefcases, T1 and T2. That made me a better, more organized person. I felt I was on my way to becoming more fully integrated, as Doctor A liked to say. Doctor A came recommended by everyone I knew, including all my nuttier clients. That was the problem. He is Toronto's pre-eminent literary psychiatrist, specializing in disorders of the creative personality. I think I read once that the Writers' Union made him an honorary life member. The trouble was I kept meeting all these people in the waiting room who were trying to sell me on something or wanted me to sell something on their behalf or to whom I owe money perhaps. As we waited there, they would tell *me* their troubles, as though I were the doctor. One of these hacks sidled up to me once to confess that he was looking for a new agent. "My old one found religion. Jesus appeared to her in a vision. He said He was coming back and wanted her to handle the publicity." Another was always complaining about his ex-wife. "She was only a lesbian long enough to get in all the anthologies."

I couldn't wait for this log-jam of broken souls to clear up so that I could get my turn inside and hear Doctor A say, "So, tell me about your dreams." He wasn't a Freudian of course, but he asked the question like a psychiatrist in a 1950s novel because I told him I liked talking about my dreams, found it helpful. Shows how old-fashioned I am. For this occasion I had memorized two dreams that he hadn't heard yet, though Doctor B (who would sometimes play along but less willingly) already knew them. In the first, a spiv approaches me while I'm waiting in the subway with my yellow briefcases.

"My name is Biscuit," he says.

For some reason, I answer, "I once killed a man named Biscuit. No relation, I suppose."

"I am the one you murdered," he says, and then he pushes me into the path of the train.

In the other dream, there is this old cop ("I'm not the janitor but the next step up") sitting on one of the stools at a diner. There are two loos. One door is marked WOMEN, the other POLICE.

But he didn't want to hear about my dreams. Instead we did a whole session on my distant ancestry. I told him the story of how, when the revolution started in 1956, Grandmother sent her man to the pawnshop with her jewellery, but not the really good stuff. That was the family story anyway. Most of the time the doctor did all the talking. On occasion my attention wandered. More than once I found myself thinking about office equipment. Back in the days when everyone was interested in telepathy, I bought my first fax machine. When I decided I wanted to be cremated, I started debating whether to get a paper shredder.

I should have got one sooner.

The Sylvia Hotel, 18 June 01

JOHN BURNS[†]

George Fetherling and I met, properly met, over drinks in the Sylvia Hotel one summer. This must have been 2001. (I guessed on that date—I'm not the one who keeps journals—but then I checked George's gifts to me from that occasion and confirmed it: "For John Burns, this odd little book, George. 18 June 01." He's turned my library into a journal without my noticing, which doesn't surprise me.) George was there, one eye fixed on the improbable beauty of English Bay, because he'd finally followed through on a resolve begun sometime in the 1960s, when he started his habit of pilgrimages to the West Coast's "urban monastic silence." After all those years, he'd left Toronto, settled on Vancouver as somewhere he could live. So it was only natural that we'd be having drinks in the Sylvia, the place exhibiting the kind of rundown gentility that appeals to him.

We talked for a couple of hours, enough to satisfy him that I was indeed as wet behind the ears as he'd imagined. I did, however, have two things in my favour, which guaranteed we'd keep up. I may not be well read but I do read a lot, and this is not unimportant

[†] John Burns is book review editor and managing editor of the *Georgia Straight* in Vancouver.

to George, who himself reads an astonishing amount, and for the most laudable of reasons: self-improvement. More to the point, I had the good grace to apologize for foolish remarks I wrote down about him at a time when my ears were even damper than they are now.

I had occasion to appreciate the enormity of this gaffe of mine, which all began in a Swiss restaurant of his acquaintance way back when he was still called Douglas, after I read a series of interviews with him published by Joe Blades's Broken Jaw Press. As we left the Sylvia that afternoon, George handed me the book, called *Jive Talk*; he'd inscribed it, as above, and because of that fact and because it was just a slip of a thing, I read it that very evening.

In *Jive Talk*, George and Blades range widely, as do the other contributors, over terrain familiar to anyone who has followed George's colossal output, particularly his two terrific books of memoirs covering, separately, the 1960s and 1970s. One passage stood out for me and has become as good a credo as I've yet found for the practice of book-reviewing: "I've reviewed books constantly since I was a teenager, as a means of continuing my education, of keeping up with what's being written and published, and as a way of being a party to the larger discourse. My rule of thumb is to be kinder to others than they are to me, hoping (vainly for the most part) that someone will notice the good example. No, that makes me sound sanctimonious, which I hope I'm not. I guess what I mean to say is that only sophisticated readers make surefooted reviewers."

The day we first had lunch, and this I can pinpoint as early March 1998, we were talking about another George, George Woodcock, whose commitment to politics and literature we both admired. In the role of The Fledgling, I was paying scant attention to the content of our talk, trying instead to fix in my mind how the bones of George, aka Douglas, aka The Older & Better, might later appear in print.

"He leaves a memory, not with his face or his body, but with his voice," I subsequently claimed. "His speech, measured, hesitant [...] picks its way deliberately through complete paragraphs. His sentences mostly begin with *And*. Though I do recall him physically—slightly twisted in his seat to favour his good ear, eyes drawn into the middle distance when I succeed in asking a question that engages his thoughtful curiosity, mouth goldfishing to overcome an intermittent stutter, and wound in a complex defence of dark sweaters and multi-pocketed vest that causes him, when he finally stands to say goodbye in trench coat and hat, to appear exactly like the kind of man who might travel the world by tramp steamers, which he has just done for his next book—it is not his image, but the cadence of his reminiscences, that lingers."

This was all, of course, twaddle.

The *Globe and Mail*'s Kate Fillion, in an interview around the publication of *Travels by Night* a few years earlier, extracted a more meaningful sample of the demons that drive him: "'She got one who couldn't talk,'" she quotes George as saying, meaning his mother and his own stuttering childhood self. "'Her response to that was to feel that she had failed and this manifested itself in violence, to the extent that you could distinguish that from the fact that she was an alcoholic for most of her life.'"

George, recalling my callow reduction of his stutter, his painful sloughing of his American background and his general self, suffered my three-years-late apologies with gentlemanly grace. I, meanwhile, shivered through a moment's epiphany. Be kind to others. In print. In person. *Remember this.*

You may be wondering why I pick at the last leavings of an old scab. Perhaps I don't want the wound to heal invisibly. Perhaps I worry at the memory of my dismay so that it will stick in my mind. Because George, through example and through his writing, has taught me things worth remembering, things about sophistication, about surefootedness. When a book review goes well—when there is more to say than space could ever accommodate and sentences offer themselves with the rhythmic regularity of vines just waiting to swing me hand over hand through the jungle—what a delight it is to read and to write. When a book review is going badly, however, and there is little to say though the screen waits for the words that will only, and at best, damn with faint praise, I think of him.

I think of George's belief in the power of the craft, a power that travels both outward and in. From *Travels by Night*: "They didn't know it, but I used literary sections of papers and magazines to subsidize my studies while earning myself a pittance in the bargain (a kind of student loan, doled out fifty or seventy-five dollars a throw, which never had to be paid back). As time went on, I grew more not less ambitious in reviews, until I thought nothing of reading four or five other books if necessary to deal adequately with the one at hand, and I came to dislike reviews that attempted to slide by on a reviewer's subjective opinion—book good, me like; book bad, me no like—without always comparing every possible facet to that of some other book or writer and without trying to deal with ideas. No reviews without ideas, this almost became a battle cry."

I think of George's best defence. From *Jive Talk*: "I honestly try to be nicer to everybody else than they are to me. Not out of altruism, out of purely selfish motives of making myself feel better. And some people, by their nastiness, make it much easier for me to be nicer to them than they are to me."

I think of George's sleeper wit, which saves him from excessive propriety. May it lend me something similar. Three out of *Notes From a Journal: 1978–1980* (published hors de commerce):

"Everything I've written is an evasion or an apology."

"Only mistake I never made consistently was being paralysed with fear at the thought of making mistakes."

"One starts out an arrogant youth and grows more and more modest until there's nothing left at all."

Notes on Fetherling's
"Our Man in Utopia"

W.H. New[†]

1. Variorum

In 1985 (when he was still writing as Douglas Fetherling), George Fetherling published a collection of forty "New Poems and Old, 1965–1985" under the title *Variorum*. The word *variorum* is aptly chosen. Generally, of course, it refers to an edited collection of texts, one that draws attention to variants in form—line, language, sequence, font—from one appearance to another. As though to stress this *effect* (although Fetherling does not strictly adhere to the editorial *practice* implied by the term), seven of the individual poems are entitled "Notation." They raise such topics as child death and its relation to the unequal distribution of the world's wealth ("each day / he lived / someone else lived one day / less"), and they work by means of statements and images: defining "weeds," reconstructing skeletons, exploring the rarity of straight lines and the attachment of poems, both metaphorically and literally, to

---

[†] W.H. New is emeritus professor of English at the University of British Columbia where he edited the journal *Canadian Literature* for seventeen years. He is the author of *A History of Canadian Literature* (1989, revised 2003) and editor of the *Encyclopedia of Literature in Canada* (2002), among many other books.

margins. Recurrent motifs in the book include many topics that characterize Fetherling's work as a whole: his analyses of Canadian social history, his wide reading in European literature, his admiration of George Woodcock's intellectual anarchism as a literary model, his engagement with the visual arts, his ventures into travel writing (which are at the same time ventures into the self) and his delight in anecdote, skill at phrasing and fascination with the borderland between self and other, particularly as revealed through landscape, nature at large, cultural difference and systems of cultural expression. While *Variorum* thus constitutes one way to read into Fetherling's large body of work, it also reveals (perhaps especially to those readers who know him best as an articulate and absorbing journalist) his remarkable skills as a poet. This work displays a mastery of subdued tone, an ear for pacing, a wit, intelligence, and a serious blend of personal insight (sometimes expressing private tribulation) with public conscience. The title invites (as a kind of reader's companion) some version of notes and commentaries, and that is what I am proposing here. Rather than track all earlier versions of each collected poem, however, I wish to look at the book as an internal variorum—a text within which the collected poems constitute variants of each other, and so function as commentaries, as the poet's dialogue with society, ideas and his own responses to society and ideas—a dialogue in which the reader is invited to take part.

2. Our Man in Utopia

At the heart of *Variorum* is a poem called "Our Man in Utopia" whose twelve irregular "stanzas" I take as signs of the book's repeated concerns and overall achievement. The poem—ostensibly a set of observations of Utopia which "our man" sends away "by bearer" to his readers—is open to various interpretations. Even the number twelve might therefore be significant (a "year's" worth of meditations, as it were, or of cryptic messages for reader-disciples). A Christian reading might emphasize the isolation of the truth-teller (the poem's meditative but anonymous narrator) in a world that seems to be at once his own and foreign, and which is said to be governed by the inadequate absolutes of material (political, military, authoritarian) power. A Zen reading is equally possible, for withdrawal from the material world seems to be hazarded as a distinct possibility in these circumstances—but the reasons for withdrawal that are expressed here (escape from responsibility? from choice? from the demand to face truth or embrace love?) might well undermine its effectiveness as a way of achieving enlightenment. Detachment, here, is not taken to be unmistakably admirable. And in any event the poem's title suggests a much more obvious dimension. A clear allusion to Graham Greene's *Our Man in Havana*, the poem calls "truth" itself into question. For Greene's novel (a satire of British postwar intelligence-gathering practices) elucidates how gathering or delivering "information" in certain kinds of hierarchical or corporate structures turns into a system of providing truths-that-are-expected rather than truths-with-a-basis-in-reality. Through witty exaggeration of incompetence and deception, Greene exposes the politics of an institutional system that thrives on suspicion and fear. But by extension, if no truth-teller (or poet?) is able to affect the powers-in-charge, then inadequacy can take hold of a society's structures and so undermine social values. Anger is sometimes a writer's way of exposing such anomie; wit is yet another. For Fetherling, both modes of expression have their place in *Variorum*; the aim appears not, however, to be direct reform, but rather an indirect engagement of the reader in understanding the disparity between an acceptance of the status quo and some other (moral, social, personal) possibility.

3. The streets are full of soldiers
 one dare not risk drunkenness so often as at home

The poem opens by expressing three kinds of anonymity—of place, person, voice—specifying neither who is observing the soldiers ("one"), nor where "Utopia" is (or at least where it is being observed). The soldiers are a uniform mass; the streets are undifferentiated. This Utopia is nowhere, and if apparently not a "better" place (*eutopia*), is it at least not "home." But what does this tell us about home, where "drunkenness" (the freedom not to conform? the possibility of a looser tongue?) is less of a "risk"? The word "so" is important. Even at home, it suggests, departures from existing norms are risky—for the poet, or for anyone who sees society from an unconventional angle.

4. Instead, in fearful contemplation
 one keeps to one's rooms which lighted
 are no safer than the boulevards in darkness

What, then, the poem asks, are the alternatives? "Instead" raises a logical expectation. But this is a world where apparent difference creates no difference, a world in which authority constructs the only acceptable option or in which some version of sameness has been misidentified as equality. The narrator remains "one," distanced from society but distanced also from himself, as though to protect whatever remnants of individual identity remain intact. And the "rooms" in which the narrator lives reveal that here there is no distinction between light and darkness, or between out and in. This inability to distinguish between light and dark *could* be read as "melancholy" (which is the word used in the few critical comments that mention this book), and melancholy might well be taken to express a narrator's personal ("fearful") depression. Perhaps. But "Our Man in Utopia" suggests that this inability to make distinctions is as much a consequence of an accepted frame of (social) reference as of any private despair. These lines do not read as inevitability; they read as circumstance, which challenges the narrator to find other ways to speak. The word "no" in line 5 echoes the "so" of line 2; in both instances, the syntactic structure is comparative rather than absolute. Resolution remains apart.

5. *The charges of the state's police*
have in practice the force they lack in foundation

The aurality of these lines—the assonance and alliteration—intensifies their effect. The word "charges" echoes "boulevards in darkness" and suggests how darkness manifests itself—arbitrarily—through social power. The words "police," "practice" and "force" connect into a subversive hiss; the flat *a* sounds that associate "have" with "practice," "lack" (and "capital" in the line following) re-emphasize the social failure to distinguish between opposites (*having* and *lacking* become the same—though not for the narrator, who can, a reader infers, still differentiate). The alliteration that links "force" with "foundation" invites the reader (as it perhaps does the ordinary denizen of Utopia) to assume a substantive association between the two words, and thus gives credence to "force," but "foundation" (echoing "contemplation" from line three) moves away from "force" and in a different direction, perhaps towards an alternative (if still inchoate, unexpressed) possibility. A further paradox is apparent: if this *is* Utopia, where all things are perfect, why is an alternative necessary? The answer lies in another conundrum: the logic of alternatives is that any contemplation of them always exposes the inadequacy of all claims upon the perfection of any social organization (*always, all, any*: words to be contemplated).

6. *In the capital it is now a crime to be naked*
   and they say this is gaining favour
                                    in the provinces
     as well

The alliteration of "capital" and "crime" reveals a hidden, carefully crafted legal pun, which tells that the death of alternatives is at least the covert desire of a power that rejects the legitimacy of opposition. "Naked" provides such opposition; the word has to be heard as a willingness to be exposed—less to disrobe than to draw attention to oneself as a voice of alternatives, which is therefore deemed to be dangerous: not in itself (though that will be the argument one hears from authority, the faceless "they") but to the authority's claim upon worthiness, respect. The physical space that follows the word "favour" has to be read as another word in these lines—as a contemplative silence, a duration in which a spatial alternative ("provinces" as distinct from "capital") is also recognized to make no difference. "Provinces," of course, is a general term for any group of sub-areas in a hypothetical social totality; yet the specific use of the term here hints that Fetherling might well be thinking of Canada as the pretend-Utopia where artistry finds it hard to voice difference.

7. *Yesterday some artisans were tried for being poor,*
   found guilty, their sentence kept a secret

Here the legal metaphor continues, and so does the textual punning: "tried" for being *true* perhaps, or judged (reviewed irrationally?), or subjected to tribulation (poverty) because art is not intrinsically valued. Writers' words, moreover—the "sentences"—are secret because unread, not just because they might be withheld, though both interpretations are possible: a covert comment on the power of publishers to accept and distribute the avant-garde or to adhere to convention might be implied.

8. *For death I have heard a person*
   can be posthumously indicted
   his body exhumed to lie before the judges
   whose faces are hidden from no one knows whom

History and literary history continue to overlap. If history is the narrative written by the winners in any conflict, then its version of value lasts only so long as those who hold power continue to be able to make the same discriminations and to exert such power. But in *practice* (that word again), historical and literary judgments continue to alter, as the relevance (to the present) of any one set of interpretations alters with changes in circumstance, taste, fashion, perspective and other criteria. Such practices have implications: in aesthetics, as in ethics, is there no such thing as absolute value (another version of Utopia)? If relative evaluation is discounted, are aesthetic (and ethical) alternatives unnecessary? Is judgment simply a matter of isolating a writer's nearness to a version of the ideal? What criteria govern judgment in any event? If (with a process of evaluative change) actual personal reputations suffer, what version of ethics governs respect—and what criteria will be used to assess those who in the present do the judging? The phrase "no one knows whom" applies in this poem to both the hidden-faced judges and those for whom they ostensibly judge; once again Fetherling's words reveal differences that make no distinctions in this Utopia. Or is a reader intended (as with Greene's *Havana*) to ask a different question: is "our man" (the narrator making the observations) the honest observer, or is he the deceiver of those who would deceive?

Is he himself to be discounted, not as a man but as a truth-teller? The poem circles back to an implied claim upon individual freedom—freedom from convention, social enclosure: the narrator in this stanza admits for the first time to the pronoun "I." Yet these lines do not indicate how this conclusion might be reached. For now, only the aural echoes, and the wit, nod towards possibility.

9. *Statues of old heroes are replaced almost daily*

The poem's wit is expressed most openly here, in figurative form, the observation (and the absurdity it carries) emphasized visually by the fact that space surrounds the stanza's single verse. Here, not only does the line affirm that old statues are replaced, it also emphasizes that replacement is a continuous action. Hence no hero is heroic for long; no value withstands time (as measured by political or aesthetic fashion). And (though the "almost" performs a sardonic cautionary role in the sentence) the phrasing is referentially absolute, for the line refers to no particular set of statues ("*the* statues" in a particular public square, say) but to "Statues" in general, with no discriminating article. They "are replaced" passively, moreover, without reference to whoever is responsible. No one *takes* responsibility, it seems—a reality that involves Utopia's citizens, and the speaker as well.

10. *The man on the street or rather of the shadows*
does not know when to wave and cheer and when
to look away

And perhaps Utopia's citizens do not take responsibility because they do not know how to do so; they occupy the shadows because it is safer not to be identifiable, because the "streets" (as stanza 1 affirmed) belong to the soldiers. But in these circumstances, what does knowledge consist of? The answer for the ordinary citizen of Utopia (the ostensibly representative "man on the street" who is consulted for statistical polls and conventional interviews) is how to be safe, how to conform, not how to oppose or how to rebel. But for "our man" the narrator, knowledge is something else: maybe the self-sufficiency to affirm what he actually does think rather than what convention or statistics dictate that he should think. Such visibility brings danger with it, a charge of idiosyncrasy perhaps, or outright dismissal (whether by argument or innuendo), or the indirect pressure conveyed by a caveat against those others who might be associated with him. This is a poem about being a writer, especially a writer with an alternative point of view in a society that works as much by connection and coterie as by sensitivity to language or innovation. It is also, continuingly, a poem about the totalitarianism of any absolutist system (whether political, religious, legal, aesthetic or any other category of organization) that governs social expectation and practice.

11. *Friends' salutations are guarded*
the once-public buildings patrolled

The consequence of fear is suspicion; the consequence of suspicion is fear. Uncertainty could encourage creativity, but in the circular climate of suspicion and fear it breeds only more suspicion, more fear and a more elaborate system of authoritarian order, which functions to preserve itself (and the climate that invites it into existence) as much as (or perhaps more than) to defend those whom once it *served*.

12. *The price on my head is commensurate with*
    the value of truths I send by the bearer

So how should the poem close? These lines ask the reader to read our man's message and evaluate it: to give it credence or to dismiss its relevance to "our" person, our world. The poet—the "bearer" of the message—is, like any messenger, as likely to be attacked as is the message itself. Hence to send the message at all is a dangerous act. As any real poem is. And the greater the "truths," the greater the danger. There is a "price" on the narrator's head, he says, adapting a pop-culture legal cliché to a world where the language of statistical, commercial, *measurable* ("commensurate") bottom-line evaluations of worth can easily take precedence over those that derive from ethical and aesthetic insights. Such a recognition should not, I think, be equated simply with "melancholy"; "Our Man in Utopia" is no mere evocation of a moment of emotional distress, but rather a figurative evocation of how opposing mindsets (the authoritarian, the relative, the passive, the oppositional) compete for readers' understanding and for readers' engagement with words. Fetherling speaks not only about the words of poetry, but also about the words of governance, the words of declared belief, the words of acceptance and refusal, exposition and demand, suspicion and irony, literalism and fear: all different, and yet, because they remain interconnected, all one. A Utopia of a different order entirely.

13. *Notation #1*

I have suggested that "Our Man in Utopia" articulates motifs that *Variorum* contemplates in other ways, among them the motifs of the traveller, the poet's role (and the image of the poet as a drowned man), the freedom of the mind to wander, the fascination of the theatre of illusion, the exigencies of poverty, the uncertainty of history, the quest for "truth" and the reliance on wit as a means of dealing with distance. Examples occur everywhere in the text, and need not be rehearsed in detail here. The traveller in "Western Manitoba" contemplates the disappearance of the border between land and sky, seeks safety from the oppressions of the forest, but constructs himself as a skeleton on the way to a fixed point on the horizon. On the shore in "Waterfront" the speaker imagines the dock as "amputated," the external world reflecting an internal sense of limitations. "Alleycat" observes that "the shortest path / between two points [is] indistinct / in the night"—and that the origin of observation (which appears to come out of "nowhere"—Utopia again) is unidentifiable. In "Christie Pits in Autumn," "some old quarries fill / with water, this one fills /with shadow." "Border Catechism" deals with destinations, "Subroutine" with burial at sea, "The Dark Grid" with the anonymity of poverty and hunger: at "the back doors / of restaurants," "no one has received / any mail in years / though you may write me if you wish / in care of the pigeons." Urban settings predominate: cities as parodies of themselves ("Nights Passed on Ward's Island, Toronto Harbour"), the "surefooted / progress of decay" that "The Six O'clock News from Buffalo" takes delight in reporting, the "sharks" who wait on tables in "Harry's New York Bar in Paris." "Rough Night at the Hotel Nonpareil" evokes sleeplessness and preoccupation with a set of vivid portraits of thieves and others, those whom society has displaced. And throughout, especially in the seven "Notations" with their repeated images of the poet as weed, skeleton, born to be drowned, the poems evoke an individual speaker, an "I" who observes the contradictions in his society and within himself and wrestles his way less towards resolution than towards an admission: that disparities are the norm, not necessarily to be accepted because of that—anger and wit convey the contrarian's impatience with lassitude—but acknowledged, no longer lied about, no longer disguised.

14. *Notation #2*

The arc that *Variorum* follows is not that of the conventional journey from youth to age or despair to revelation; instead, the repetitions and variations, the interplay of motifs, convey how meditative dialogues work. They range over and over a territory of ideas—social disparities and individual options, aesthetic conventions and artists' roles, perceived inadequacies and annotations of alternative possibilities—and in accumulation they articulate the mind's progress through affirmation, negation, confrontation and imagination. The opening poem, "Prologue," asks what happens when people abandon nature. The tentative answer is that nature abandons people, and the poem works its way through a syntax of negation towards its affirmation of the need to see: "This is not the apocalypse, it is / not even morning / but only a reminder / of what's obvious and basic." *Seeing*, however, remains a challenge. As "Elijah Speaking" observes, "I have lived in focus scarcely at all / for as a child I knew I was no child / as now I know I am not old." *Knowing*, in turn (as "Our Man in Utopia" reaffirms), is as problematic as seeing, and it is a challenge to negotiate a way through (or among) competing versions of truth. "Poem Beginning with a Title from Philip Lamantia" [Lamantia, b. 1927, the American avant-garde poet] poses this challenge in yet another way: as one of reconciling "ancient" traditions with such contemporary realities as tattoos (the poem dates from before tattoos became middle-class fashion), urban shantytowns and black revolvers in ordinary people's hands.

15. *Notation #3*

Two long poems from the first half of *Variorum* further this ongoing meditation on poetry's status and function in current society. "The Hours of Old Elijah" (terce, nones, vespers) begins with a reflection on the "deficit living" of the present moment, goes on to regret despair and to wish for the grace to "study time, not catalogue it," but ends acknowledging time's continuing (and deceptive) effect on perception: "Soon I shall be history / Already my habits have become traditions / and my memories the facts / I am . . ./ unable to give shade as I once did." Mere appeals to "tradition" have to be examined, but at this point in the poem, no clear analysis immediately follows. The speaker ("our man" again) awaits "your instructions," seeking (paradoxically) both someone to read him and someone to write him into direction. A second three-part poem, "Teratology" (the term refers to the branch of medicine that treats "abnormality and monstrosity"), picks up on the drowned poet motif ("the outlaw grows accustomed / to living / without future tenses"). Alluding to a range of mentors (Blake, De Quincey, Corvo: "masochistic wisemen"), the poem then confronts the sexuality of the poet's relations with landscape and time, and tries to identify why in modern times the poet (by this time generalized from an individual figure into a way of seeing the world) seems to have died: others find him in an alley, "in a see-through shroud / dead of multiple allusions / starved of his own traditions / by hearsay / innuendo / asphyxiated by everyone else's. . . ." But any "archaeologist" at the morgue, the poem concludes, will nevertheless be afraid of what he will discover. *Variorum* thus returns again to considering why a culture of fear so bedevils the world—particularly the fear that individuals feel when put in a position of confronting themselves. Poetry, these poems affirm, asks us to look at who and where we are, to see enough to begin to sort out what and how we know. "Our Man in Utopia," in other words, is us.

16. *Notation #4*

It is fitting, then, that *Variorum* should close with a poem called "Contributor's Note," which at once follows convention and breaks it. Wittily adapting the habitual paradigms of criticism, news journalism and book jacket practice, the poem consists of twenty-six statements, each a form of identification for "the author." These range from "The author wishes to remain anonymous" (the evasive ploy), "The author is a figment of our collective imagination" (the Jungian formula) and "The author isn't bad just misunderstood" (the sociological excuse) cumulatively through the punning metaphor "The author is an open book," to the allusively political and definitely past-tense twinned observations "The author was mentioned in dispatches / The author was always in the line of fire." Like "Our Man in Utopia" in other words—though our man himself might never have known if his observations were received or if he was ever sent a reply. But the poems in *Variorum,* taken together, function rather like the message our man gives to his bearer: knowing that the "actual" outcome is indeterminable, they nevertheless seek communication. George Fetherling himself has gone on from *Variorum* to inquire many more times into writing and social behaviour. How to communicate the dilemma of "Our Man in Utopia" remains for him a continuing artistic and intellectual challenge. His poems call upon the reader to try to locate values in a civil society—to try to find the civility of society—perhaps especially when habits are taken as truths, cliché is mistaken for thought, violence intrudes into ordinary lives and fear prevails.

First Signs of Anarchist Spring[†]

George Fetherling

Eleven ships in English Bay this morning
impatient for their turn at the gantries
ten or more every day so far this month
business in China must be good
cherry blossoms underfoot like confetti
once the echoes evaporate
I leave my footprints until the next breeze.

Americans have a new war
that's how we know the generations have changed
but we're not headlines we don't need verbs
to validate ourselves.
To the east, the shoulder of the sky is hunched
in back of the sun, still arguing for acceptance
begging us to go there.
The strategy is to let the future emerge
a little at a time that we might grow accustomed
and not protest or go mad.
The window opens so briefly that we cannot
throw out the words.
This will have to do for now.

[†] Previously unpublished.

Mountains to the north zoom in
on people currently between destinations
it's time to harvest the lessons
tomorrow is deep yesterday shallow
sometimes the other way round.
Be like the cave-dwelling hermit
who learns from the mute and mocks
the big yellow bruise.
Slideshow over, the screen goes white
we revert to ritual avoidance of rituals
as practised by lordly bureaucrats who seldom
deviate from what they receive.
The meaningless courage of the entourage
fails them as usual.
Dawn dusk inhale exhale
at night when the stars tremble
we will have no comfort to offer
consumed as we are in events we observe
yet refuse to follow.

Old before my time in relation
to the time available
I spend my declining years declining to accept
struggling to continue trusting the voice
that is the public function of the heart.
In the end, succour finds its own level
everyone fingers everybody else
everyone forgives everybody else
we're all subsidiaries of one another
whatever I know I've learned by
eavesdropping.

George Fetherling's *Selected Poems*: An Appreciation

George Elliott Clarke[†]

Following *Variorum: New Poems and Old 1965–85*, which appeared in 1985, George Fetherling issued a second selection of his poetry, *Selected Poems*. That was in 1994, an anagram of his birth year, 1949. I mention this fact for I am sure it did not go unnoticed by the poet, a man whose belles-lettres are infatuated with coincidences, odds and ends of information, biographical accidents, historical quirks and occult politics. Fetherling is our principal poet of the archive, of marginalia, of illuminated obscurities. No wonder he is a consummate compiler, a pack rat of erudition who can leap nimbly from cataloguing assassins and accounts of their plots and victims (*The Book of Assassins*, 2001) to composing a zesty, allusive and moving elegy for his father (*Singer, An Elegy*, 2004). Clearly, the ideal employment of his temperament was his editing of the journal *Canadian Notes & Queries*, which permitted him to treat all of literature as a master library of provocative disclosures, tantalizing trivia and Sphinx-like silences.

[†] George Elliott Clarke's many works include *Execution Poems*, which won the Governor General's Award in 2001, and the novel *George & Rue* (2005). He teaches at the University of Toronto.

Presumably, Fetherling's encyclopaedic compulsion is the consequence of his autodidact experience. In English-Canadian poetry, he shares this "primitive" or "naïve" pedigree with go-your-own-way figures like Gwendolyn MacEwen (once his lover), Al Purdy, Anne Szumigalski and George Woodcock, all writers who valued independence, a distrust of the academy (while valuing its occasional supports) and, ultimately, mystical beliefs. (Fetherling's own mysticism resides, arguably, in the notion that Truth can be excavated through an anatomizing of reality, a rigorous indexing of its published manifestations.)

In *Selected Poems*, his seining of some thirty years of publication dating back to 1965, when as a sixteen-year-old he wrote the first poem he found to have been a "keeper," Fetherling showcases the obstinate yet varied nature of his obsessions, from finding "Gandhi, Christ, Li Po, and Lee Harvey Oswald" (*Selected*, 140) equally compellingly charismatic, to worrying the divide between craft (newspapers and orthography) and art (chapbooks and fonts). Revealingly, he avers in his author's note that "[f]rom the start, I was a political and religious poet (in that order), and so I have remained" (ibid). These overlapping identities—with their echoes of mentor Dennis Lee, *frère* Anglo-Canadian nationalist George Grant and anarcho-patriot Woodcock—inform the rhythms and High Red Tory philosophy and sardonic clarity of Fetherling's epigrammatic poems. (For further information on his predilections, see Fetherling's bestseller *Travels By Night: A Memoir of the Sixties*, 1994.) The lyrics also exude a Greco-Roman classicism, valuing incisive description over the charms of sensual pictorialism. To define a world where, in Marx's formulation, "everything solid melts into air," Fetherling utilizes a language that is democratic, vernacular and expansive but also exact, uncompromising and verifiable. He is the Tom Paine of poetry, in the sense of being a lyric pamphleteer who prefers aphorism to metaphor.

His rhetorical *ars poetica* is apparent in "Western Manitoba." Here the persona remarks, "We are tearing down the highway / and above us the clouds // are like opening titles of MGM's / most spectacular film." This union of nature and commerce proves unhappy though. "The sky in the west // grows progressively bluer, [and] we are led / to expect some large celebration / when cement air and earth end together // in a point" (*Selected*, 10). This promise of future comedy, of satisfying finales, is brought up short by the memento mori image of the driver and companion as "two skeletons with maps in an old Chevrolet" (ibid). Neither American technology nor Canadian roadway, neither American Beat-vagabonding nor Canadian touring can deliver the speaker (into) the heaven vaunted by mass media and popular culture. Fetherling's Black Mountain openness of line, of attitude, affirms this reading, as does his suspicion, reinforced by the concluding image, that modern questing is merely self-indulgent self-destruction.

Similarly bleak imagery haunts "Notation #1," which must also be understood as Fetherling's commentary on his self-reportedly hateful, filial-maternal relationship:

> Above was a sign
> which read in translation
> Street of the Abortionists
> where he was pulled
> from his mother
>   who had been
> raped by all the races
> with his eyes open
> and his mouth
>   in a high
> and grotesque laugh
> the doctor tried to silence
> with a knife that came out
> black [....]

A clinical morbidity emphasizes the *Exorcist*-like sardonic humour of this natal introduction to (emotional) violence. Again, Fetherling wields classical economy to accent postmodern—but timeless—inhumanity. The poem ends:

> and each day
> he lived
> someone else lived one day
> less
>
> Foetuses in amphorae
> skeletons in cars (*Selected*, 13).

The jump-cut finale, telescoping history in two lines, reminds us that Fetherling has been a prodigious film reviewer. Rapid transitions between images, along with references to movies, are hallmarks of his poems.

"Notation #2" shows off a persona who, once more, reveals living flesh to be a laughable denial of its inevitable decline to the underlying skeletal:

> Ignorant child
> playing
> with a skull in its crib
> has no sense of its unimportance
> but pokes stubby fingers
> through eye sockets
> gurgling like a moron
> takes a delicate cobweb
> from the nasal cavity
> twirls
> it laughing around a finger
> like spaghetti [...] (*Selected*, 44).

This macabre and Gothic tone dominates Fetherling's poetry

throughout, recalling the pessimism of Grant but also that of Maine Yankee and tragic Transcendentalist Edwin Arlington Robinson. The poem concludes with the description of its Yorick-like deceased as having been "born / a skeleton [that] lived middle age / in an upstairs room / and laughed as he poured / the champagne on the roaches / that would not be drowned" (*Selected*, 44).

While Fetherling's decline-and-fall theme offers the standard frisson of despair at the glib optimism (that is, wishful thinking) of liberals, America, due to its claim of being a God-appointed paradise of communal bounty and individual liberty, is subject to special disdain. Thus in "The Six O'Clock News from Buffalo," the persona reports on "streamers" that "turned / to cobwebs" and on "waterfalls / [that] became escalators / which finally broke down // in the surefooted / progress of decay [...]" (*Selected*, 53). In another poem, the result of past American imperialism in Panama is "decay [...] a kind of pollution" now, "the principal export / chief industry, major resource // and part of our sorrow is that the sorrow's gone / leaving only tourists and derelicts behind" (*Selected*, 52). The ideal of America—hope, fresh starts, new frontiers etc.—is revealed a mask for swindles, corruption, rot and fraud: civics reduced to vices, progress become progressive decay.

Canada is not immune to this diagnosis. Again, like Grant, Fetherling depicts Canada as accepting American ideals and thus American ills that are ultimately the sicknesses of western civilization. But if Grant writes in the spirit of Jeremiah, lamenting and protesting the loss of traditional virtues and "virtuous" traditions, Fetherling adopts the mode of Ecclesiastes and Proverbs, limning the poetry of notes, asides, haiku and essay to express his clerical reservations about our collective vanities. See, for instance, his longer poem "Moving Towards the Vertical Horizon" (*Selected*, 56–73), where the speaker asserts: "Each generation believed itself / a moral and cultural advance, / that was the secret where the poison / was hidden / that was the key to organized decay…" (*Selected*,

67). Here too Fetherling's persona observes the withering away of literature itself:

> I once thought I had
> uses for novels that were
> practically trash in 1910
> and now are almost art
> grammars of decaying languages [...]
> works
> of *philosophy* well disguised
> ones that were in themselves
> *accomplishments*
> and earned their authors
> obituaries in The Times with
> remarks by ambivalent colleagues
> (*Selected*, 59–60; italics in the original).

In our time, however, the market for such works has so collapsed that "no one [reads] them but me." But with the money earned by "selling them back to /second hand dealers who got them / second hand from their rivals," the speaker purchases or fashions "a means of escape" including "a poncho that's also a hammock / and doubles as a one-person tent" (*Selected*, 60).

As an archivist, Fetherling holds dear two truths: 1) this current reality too will pass, and 2) there is nothing new under the sun. Two separate haiku-proverbs underline this point: "Tomorrow's archaeology today / the mirror's backed up again / office towers sweating" (*Selected*, 78) and "Language derives from sighs / bills of atonement / the past is legally binding" (*Selected*, 79). A third poem may yield justification for Fetherling's retrieval of forgotten or lost values, ideals and truths: "Read on / ransacking shelves / the dead leave messages in books" (*Selected*, 86). (Stranded in our sterile, chatty, yet deaf present, the persona, at the terminus of "Radio," cries out, "My dead friends / why can't I find you on the radio?" [*Selected*, 103].)

"Accumulated Wisdom," a poem consisting of more than a dozen proverbs, concludes with the one most pertinent for Fetherling: "the child who grows up shall remember" (*Selected*, 108).

In *Lament for a Nation: The Defeat of Canadian Nationalism* (1965), Grant opines, "Even on a continent [North America] too dynamic to have memory, it may still be salutary to celebrate memory" (*Selected*, 4). Like Dennis Lee in his *Civil Elegies* (1968, revised 1972), Fetherling pursues the *radical* Grantian tasks of remembering alternative systems of thought and retrieving lost truths. I am reminded of Ezra Pound's methodology and rationale in *The Cantos*. But where Pound is execrable, Fetherling is salutary: he calls on us to recall passed-on traditions—to lament those good but dead and to save those laudable and salvageable. *Selected Poems* is a vital assembly of Fetherling's prophetic—and forensic—remembrances. It proves to us what we still must hear and heed: "The dead know best" (*Selected*, 125). Amen.

From the Farmstead to the Condo: George Fetherling on Literature and Publishing in Canada

John Clement Ball[†]

JB: You've been involved in Canadian writing and publishing for about 30 years now. How would you compare the literary scene now to the one you knew back then?

GF: The whole environment is much more complex and more cosmopolitan than when I started out at Anansi in the late 1960s. One generation has grown old and respectable (well, nearly respectable in my own case) and been joined, even supplanted, by another—inevitably. In writing, the emphasis has certainly shifted from poetry to fiction during that time. In publishing, the small literary presses are more commercial than they used to be (they've had to adapt to the withering away of government arts funding) while the commercial presses are, well, more commercial—but more numerous, too. There was a time not all that long ago when the death of McClelland and Stewart—I speak of here of the

---

† John Clement Ball, who teaches at the University of New Brunswick, conducted this interview in October and November 1999. It appeared in *Studies in Canadian Literature / Études en littérature canadienne* 25:1 (2000).

company as it was under Jack McClelland's ownership—would have been a national tragedy, reported on the national news broadcasts and the front pages of the morning papers, with all the attendant apparatus of obsequies and analysis. By the middle or late 1980s that wouldn't have been the case at all, as a lot of other important players had joined in the task of publishing the important literary writers. The list of these companies changes from year to year, as the interest of their corporate owners fades in and out like a distant radio signal, but at various points the list would have to include not only the Canadian-owned Stoddart and Douglas & McIntyre but also Penguin Books Canada, Knopf Canada, Random House Canada, Doubleday Canada, HarperCollins—one could go on. In the 1960s and 1970s our fear was americanization, today it's globalization. Penguin of course is British, but Knopf, Random and Doubleday all are part of the Bertelsmann empire in Germany, while HarperCollins is whatever nationality Rupert Murdoch is projecting at the moment. Such is the present landscape. Is it better? Or worse? Well, it's different.

JB: It seems to me that Anansi—which closed for a while in the late eighties and was then reinvented in the nineties as a kind of boutique imprint of a large mainstream press—serves as a fascinating case study for some of the broader changes the industry has gone through. I see the two versions of Anansi as characteristic—perhaps even exemplary—of their times. What do you see when you compare the two?

GF: Someone—I think it was Val Ross, the publishing reporter of the *Globe and Mail*—called small literary publishers the research-and-development arm of literature. 'Twas ever thus, at least in the age of late modernity, reckoned from about the 1890s on. The original Anansi, founded in 1967, served that function superbly, if also chaotically when viewed from the inside. It gave a forum, and an audience, to talents as diverse as Peggy Atwood, Dennis Lee, Marian Engel, Dave Godfrey, Rachel Wyatt, Graeme Gibson—the list is very long. The story has been told many times (and is about to be told again by John Metcalf, who's working on a descriptive bibliography of Anansi titles). I tell it myself, as well as I can recollect it, in a book called *Travels by Night: A Memoir of the Sixties*, which has a certain following among my fellow geezers. The present Anansi is probably serving the same sort of role by publishing Esta Spalding and Steven Heighton and… again, one could go on, citing an entire directory of names. The difference is that the Anansi of old was cockily independent in ownership while the present Anansi is owned by Jack Stoddart who, in addition to his core companies, Stoddart Publishing and General Publishing, either owns or has equity in, let me see, Boston Mills Press, Cormorant, Quarry Press, Macfarlane Walter & Ross, Douglas & McIntyre and possibly others I'm forgetting. He's had to invest in these companies in order to get or keep them properly capitalized but also, I suppose, to give himself as broad a base as possible. That is to say, in an environment with so many well-fed foreign-owned houses, he's had to become a kind of smaller and Canadian-owned auto-conglomerate in order to stay competitive. But while the business functions have come together in new patterns like this, the old editorial functions—the editorial distinctiveness of each imprint—have remained the same to a degree that's remarkable in the circumstances. Or so it seems to me.

JB: You mentioned the ownership question, and the original House of Anansi was, of course, part of a group of nationalist presses that founded the Association of Canadian Publishers in 1971. The ACP has always maintained as a core policy that Canadian writing, and

Canadian culture as a whole, are best served by a strong, Canadian-owned publishing industry. Now, though, it seems the aim of
many established and new Canadian novelists is to be published
by whichever large firm offers the best arrangement, regardless of
ownership. And, of course, leading Canadian writers are aggres-
sively courted by foreign-owned publishers. So, has the ownership
question become less important now that our literature has ma-
tured, or should we be concerned that the old argument may be
falling on deaf ears?

GF: Personally, I think ownership is crucial—to some extent. If you
give up that criterion entirely, reading and writing become vassal
forms—like Canadian film. Virtually no English-Canadian feature
films—ones about actual Canadians in Canadian settings—get
made because they can't get distributed here: the Americans own
nearly all the screens, as they say in the trade, and Jack Valenti, the
head of the powerful Hollywood lobby and a former key advisor to
Lyndon Johnson during the Vietnam War, isn't going to permit any
ragtag insurgent groups to compromise him this time. Yet it's true
paradoxically that the big foreign-owned publishing houses, having more money and wishing to be good citizens, do much of the
most interesting literary publishing—of writers who've first been
brought out by the small presses (again, as of old). I guess many
writers, unlike me, are star-struck by the possibility of also being
published in New York. The problem with the foreign-owned publishers is that they have a kind of attention deficit disorder. Penguin,
to take an example, was the primary producer of interesting Canadian fiction in the 1980s but has backed away in the 1990s. In my
lifetime, McGraw-Hill has supplemented its educational publishing
by setting up a Canadian trade-publishing arm but then lost interest in a few years when New York realized that huge profits weren't
rolling in. A few years later, it's tried again. And yet again. Publish-

ing requires stamina and stubbornness. You can't be throwing out your mission statement all the time. Also, this flitting round has an effect on reading habits because it precludes reader loyalty to particular houses. Look at the railway bookstalls in Britain and you'll still see paperbacks arranged in sections according to publisher: the Penguins over here together, the Corgis over there. The same is true in France. Readers learn to depend on certain publishers to keep them supplied with what they're looking to read. This notion has never taken hold in Canada because the publishers—even the small ones—keep altering their mandates, or, in the case of the foreign-owned houses, being ordered to do so. The fact that there isn't much variety in Canadian book-design plays a role in this situation as well. Some publishers' titles are well designed (those of Insomniac Press, say, or, in a different way, Douglas & McIntyre's) while others', those of the statistical majority, are not. Virtually nobody pursues a characteristic look (much less a format) that one can spot from across a crowded bookshop.

JB: That's very interesting. I can think of some other small presses who have gone for a consistent look: Mercury Press, for instance, with their contemporary, urban-looking designs by Gordon Robertson from a few years ago; or Oberon, who have done some really ugly covers lately, though at least they have a uniform look! I wonder, though, whether those presses saw any increase in their profile and sales by doing this. McClelland and Stewart are going for a kind of series look with their recent paperback reprints, and of course have always done this with the New Canadian Library. It seems to me, though, that there are a lot of beautifully designed books out there—from publishers such as Goose Lane, Anansi, Cormorant and others—that have no brand-recognition element besides the logo on the spine. Do you think they suffer as a result, or can they get by on their reputations and the names of their authors?

GF: I'm glad you mention Gordon Robertson. He's designed three books of mine and is one of the two Canadian book designers whose work I know best (the other is Barbara Hodgson in Vancouver). Even allowing for the constant change in taste that's the essence of design, to compare these people with those who passed for designers twenty years ago is risible. Anyway, yes, I agree, there are many handsomely designed books (and yet, oddly, no conspicuous annual award for book design—this in a country that is suddenly gagging with literary awards of every conceivable sort). But I don't think individual examples of outstanding design, rather than an overall approach to design, could lead to reader loyalty and thus influence a firm's sales overall. Of course, this isn't to deny that, particularly in the case of art books and near-art books, design helps to create word-of-mouth sales, the same sort of buzz that, when applied to a literary text, can make a particular novel, say, a hot property—though I add that in my own experience and observation there's a clear difference between buzz in the media and buzz in the bookstores: the one doesn't always lead to the other.

JB: Let's move from design to editing: what do you think of the current state of literary editing in Canada? Are Canadian presses better or worse at this than they were in your early days?

GF: Generally better, once you make allowance for the problems that accompany the new technologies and the general lowering of literacy. Bev Daurio of Mercury Press, which you mentioned a moment ago—certainly one of the most serious and consistently excellent small presses—told me with a sigh recently that editorial work is a dying art. As one half of what's only a two-person shop, she prefers to confine the titles that require close editorial work to the autumn, so as to give herself a lighter load with the spring books. Publishing is a business that's somehow never quite made the transition from the Julian to the Gregorian calendar: its year still begins in March, not January. In virtually every case except Mercury, this is because of the hope of high Christmas sales and the expectation of a high level of returns soon afterwards. Only at Mercury, as far as I'm aware, does it have to do with the quality and sophistication of the prose! I like that! As for the commercial houses, in recent years the tendency in editorial, just as in publicity, has been to have fewer staff with benefits and more freelancers working on a job-by-job basis. Outsourcing, as the business journalists say. This has turned some managing editors' offices into something like union hiring-halls for merchant seamen. The result has been an inevitable unevenness. When the original Coach House Press was a co-operative, I admired the way they used to list the board member who had edited the book for the press. This encouraged pride in craft rather than the hiding of blame. Predictably yet paradoxically, the most dedicated small presses, some of which publish the fewest titles, and the two biggest academic presses, University of Toronto Press and McGill-Queen's University Press, which publish the most Canadian titles, have the loftiest editorial standards. By loftiest I guess I mean most thoughtful and consistent. That's not to say that their house styles are devoid of charming eccentricities. Taking the straight-aways with the round-abouts, I'd say that Canadian books are less rewritten in-house than are US books (this applies to magazines as well—see Paul Theroux's essay on the subject) but that there's not so much freedom for the author here as there is in British publishing (which is perhaps why British books still tend not to distinguish *that* from *which*).

JB: Editing, of course, is a largely invisible craft as far as most readers are concerned. But awards and the media, which you mentioned a minute ago, can make a big difference to a book's impact. Let's start with awards: you suggested that we have seen a proliferation of these, and I agree—as we speak we're right in the middle of it, with the Giller Prize and Governor General's Award shortlists out but the winners yet to be announced. Have these prizes, and others such as the various provincial and local awards, the Commonwealth Book Prize and so on, helped raise the profile of Canadian literature in general, or do they simply benefit the particular publishers and authors that are nominated? And do we have too many awards, do you think?

GF: A while ago the Writers' Union decided to set up web pages for its members. A sort of template was included with the application. It said: "List book awards received and prizes won (please limit yourself to only five)." As someone who's never won a book prize, I felt so intimidated and ashamed that I didn't even return the questionnaire. I guess that's why I'm often asked to be a juror: no chance of a potential conflict. There are now so many literary awards for Canadians—city, provincial, regional, national, Commonwealth, international and disciplinary ones—that there's a web site that keeps track of them all. I suspect that the ones with the consistently higher standards—the BC Book Prizes, the Giller, the GGs of course, particularly in fiction, the Orange Prize and the Booker—do increase the stature and sales of the winners, maybe even of the shortlisted titles as well. But the prizes whose low standards carry over from year to year—such as the City of Toronto Book Awards—or those whose primary concerns are inoffensiveness and folksiness—the Leacock Award—bring neither prestige nor profit. The bright note about awards is that they provide a fair-sized lump of cash for writers, which is all the more necessary given the cutbacks in arts funding by the granting agencies. As a disinterested party, though, I've often felt that the winner-take-all approach is cruel. How much fairer it would be to emulate the parimutuel system of horse-racing and divide the purse into win, place and show.

JB: The media play a big part in bringing these awards to the public's attention, and a cynic might say that some awards exist only as publicity vehicles, rather than for some loftier aim of inspiring and rewarding excellence. But the media covers books in a lot of other ways. When I worked in publishing in the late 1980s, people were fond of saying that the three best ways to sell a book in Canada were "Gzowski, Gzowski, Gzowski." That wasn't completely true, of course, and with the end of CBC's *Morningside* it's certainly not the case now. As an author who also does an enormous amount of reviewing, what are your thoughts on the ways the media covers books—especially literary ones?

GF: That literary journalism is in a wretched condition is one of those statements that one can make at any point along the timeline of our lives without fear of uttering a falsehood. It's like saying that the CBC is in decline or that the railways are being unfair to farmers. One reason is that book-reviewing has always been an entry-level activity. Very few of my contemporaries (Katherine Govier comes to mind as an exception) seem to enjoy the give-and-take of the higher journalism as a normal part of the business of being a citizen-writer. Much of the blame lies with the daily newspapers. You could be sure that they would take books much more seriously if books accounted for as much advertising linage as movies do. Every author can tell you horror stories that are truly, well, horrendous. I once published a travel book about the rise of democracy in Taiwan. In one of the Toronto newspapers it was reviewed by a paid propagandist of the People's Republic, with no acknowledgement of this conflict being made anywhere. Most book reviews, even in the specialized media, are full of words such as *good* and *bad* and *like* and *dislike*: it's quite unbelievable the levels of subjective inarticulateness to which most reviewers sink. And I say this as one who's sat on both sides of the fence, having done my time as the harried book-review editor of a couple of daily newspapers. I agree with the late George Woodcock who complained to me once that a scathing review will kill the sales of a book but that a laudatory one of the same specific gravity will not elevate sales. I've reviewed books constantly since I was a teenager, as a means of continuing my education, of keeping up with what's being written and published, and as a way of being a party to the larger discourse. My rule of thumb is to be kinder to others than they are to me, hoping (vainly for the most part) that someone will notice the good example. No, that makes me sound sanctimonious, which I hope I'm not. I guess what I mean to say is that only sophisticated readers make surefooted reviewers. The number of persons who know how to approach a text qua text has probably declined significantly since the generality of people from Christian backgrounds stopped trying to make sense of the hodgepodge that is the Bible. This is not a religiously inspired statement, you understand, but simply an observation that the reading public's familiarity with various ages of prose has faded, along with their comfort level in reading texts translated from other languages. As for your question about the electronic media's coverage of books, it seems to me that they must approach publishing as a very minor part of showbiz. Television and even radio cover books on the false premise that ideas and language can be made to sound like sporting events. The call-in radio shows that so predominate in the West are the worst. No wonder that authors who do the tour are notorious among publishers for leaving behind them a single unbroken trail of empty mini-bars from one ocean to the other.

JB: I assume, then, that you're not too keen on what passes for the literary star system in the country. Lately it seems to me that beyond Atwood it's the fresh faces—the hot young (and usually Toronto-based) prospects, often first novelists—who get the fawning attention of the media, which of course is also mostly Toronto-based. Perhaps I'm just becoming hyper-conscious of this, now that I've moved from Toronto to Fredericton…

GF: Nobody *likes* Toronto. Certainly not the people who live there. Despite a good deal of decentralization in recent years, however, it *does* remain the book-publishing centre, the home of the national newspapers and so on—just as it once had a near monopoly on pork-packing. Once it was Hogtown, now it's Booktown. This in itself signifies no improvement in the city as a place to lead daily lives nor in the sophistication of its citizenry. If my meagre resources would permit, I would live full-time, rather than just for stretches, in BC, because that's where the creative juice is—a much different commodity than publishing pull. Or, if not Vancouver, then possibly Amsterdam. I don't know anyone in Amsterdam and no one knows me. But I seem to be the spitting image of about seventeen percent of its adult male population, thus making it very difficult for anyone to give the police an accurate description of me.

JB: Agents, presumably, have something to do with the hype that's out there. But they're also helping some writers, including a few brand-new ones, make some good money. Is the rise of the literary agent in the1990s having a good or a bad overall impact on writing and publishing in Canada?

GF: Big-time, big-talking agents came to Canada comparatively
late in the day—the late 1980s. That's a century, nearly, after Conrad was represented by the famous J.B. Pinker (while his friend
Ford Madox Ford came to be handled by David Higham). In New
York, the agent was an indispensable part of the equation in the
1920s. But in Canada it was possible for a writer (I offer myself as
a typical example) to be unagented until the early 1990s, because
the community was small enough that one could know or at least
have met everyone of importance. I once spent a day at what were
then called the Public Archives of Canada looking at the cartons
containing the records of the first Macdonald government. So little
paperwork, so small a bureaucracy. I daresay Sir John A. probably
knew everyone of the remotest importance in, for example, the post
office department. Similarly, I knew all the publishers and editors a
dozen years ago. Now that's no longer possible, not even remotely.
Another thing about agents—I find this comes up frequently in
workshops and seminars—is that non-professional writers misun-
derstand the agent's role almost totally. The function of the agent
is not as it's shown in that awful early 1960s movie *Youngblood
Hawke,* based I believe on an equally awful Herman Wouk novel,
in which the literary agent, played by Suzanne Pleshette, solves the
personal problems of her promising young client author, portrayed
by someone like Troy Donahue. The job of the agent is to field
offers, negotiate contracts and collect amounts owing, in exchange
for fifteen percent of the book so long as it remains in copyright.
That's actually quite a good deal for the recidivist writer who
produces a steady body of work. Without an agent, such a person
might easily find herself losing fifteen percent of her book income
to weak negotiation and another fifteen percent to bad debts. So
to pay an agent fifteen percent in order to gain thirty percent is a
blessing. A publisher may be able to play fast and loose with an individual author but not with an agent, since there are perhaps only
twenty or so important ones at any given time and they represent a

rather high proportion of the pool of publishable authors. But the main reason that agents exist is that the publishers, who are business executives, are glad to pay a few more dollars (the increase is passed on to the consumer anyway) for the comfort of dealing with another businessperson rather than with someone they perceive as an egotistical bohemian know-nothing. My experience is that few publishers *like* writers much, as a sociological type.

JB: Could you comment on the current state of bookselling in this country, and the effect it's having on our writers and publishers—especially the rise of Chapters and the Internet booksellers?

GF: The ruination of independent bookselling by Chapters (Indigo is not only much smaller but seems less voracious) has been a tragedy for this country equal to if not surpassing the decline of the press into gossip and other trivialities. The public think they're getting a bargain but the extra discounts that Chapters is able to squeeze out of its suppliers, the publishers, are simply passed along to the customers as higher book prices, which puts people off. At a time when the national inflation rate is, what?, about two percent give or take, the annual inflation rate on retail book prices is—I can't begin to calculate. Certainly a far, far higher figure. This helps no one. As for electronic bookselling, Amazon.com is certainly a great *American* resource, though I fear that it's dissipating its usefulness by selling too many other types of merchandise in addition to books. The Canadian equivalents, which should be the most accurate and up-to-date sources of information about Canadian titles, are not up to snuff. I looked myself up on the Chapters site not long ago and found several books that are years out-of-print listed as "shippable in 24 hours," ones in-print called "no longer available," several non-existent books attributed to me, one book written by someone else attributed to me and one I'd written alone (my second volume of memoirs, in fact) listed as a collaboration between me and my friend Christopher Moore, the chair of the Writers' Union, who of course had no hand in the book whatsoever. Such a site is not only worthless as a bibliographical or reference tool, I can't see how it can be that helpful to the bookselling business. To be fair, this is a new (and huge) undertaking. Bugs are inevitable. But imagine a source of information even less accurate than the old *Canadian Books in Print*! If the Chapters people were smart they would poll Canadian writers, asking for corrections. No doubt the situation will be fixed by the time this interview appears in print.

JB: Uh, sure, if you say so. Of course, by then Y2K may have confounded everything even further, and maybe they'll be attributing the collected works of Douglas Adams to you. (I suppose you wouldn't mind that if you also got his royalties...) You sound gloomy about the independents, but surely there's still a place for hands-on booksellers who actually select their stock personally, know their books and their customers well and who host readings and launches and book clubs and the like. We have a couple of fine independents in Fredericton, and though we've now got a Chapters, the smaller stores seem to be holding their own and keeping their customers.

GF: The surviving independents are society's true heroes, like single mums. But the trend seems to be for only the most specialized to prosper—those dealing exclusively in travel books, say, or art books or cookery books. I think the general independent bookseller faces a rough future unless, as some experts have suggested in the press, Chapters has already reached a saturation point in terms of the number of sites. But then of course Chapters, in turn, is as much threatened by the larger online booksellers as the independent shops are by the so-called big-box megastores. As CEOs like to say in their annual messages inside annual reports, "It has been a year of transition."

JB: All these recent developments we've talked about—in book-selling, design, reviewing, awards, marketing, agenting, ownership and so on—are they having an impact on the kind of writing and reading being done in this country? Are these various contexts affecting Canadian literature in any ways general enough to be called trends?

GF: I believe you would have to say that some of them are *supporting* certain trends, such as that of Canadian fiction writers especially to reach out beyond Canada's borders. This is guesswork on my part, but I would suggest that the foreign audience now reads Canadian literature for its urbanity or urbanness rather than for its reflection of mock-wilderness, as of old, in the great arc that stretched from the very beginnings to Grey Owl to Farley Mowat. An older generation of, for instance, Germans, may still read such fur-bearing stuff, but a different age group is now eagerly consuming Anne Michaels or Evelyn Lau, to take merely two names that pop into mind. They do so in search of shared sensibilities rather than some idealized vision of the frontier. Mind you, whenever I've received one of those dreaded calls from Foreign Affairs to ask if I'll have lunch with a visiting Estonian poet or Armenian playwright, the question the visitor is most likely to ask is, "Why do I see none of your aboriginal people on the streets when the streets themselves, and most of the towns and rivers, have aboriginal names?" (Answering this is a long process.) And also, as I've said often before, Canadian lit fares very well indeed as part of British and Commonwealth lit (perhaps the only field in which the Commonwealth might be said to have genuine tangible worth). Yet, paradoxically, Canada thrives cultur-ally within such a group because (in my crackpot theory of the universe) it is the only economically large nation whose literature has gone from the rural to the postmodern without (a few indi-vidual exceptions—mostly in Montreal—notwithstanding) passing through the age of urban industrialization. The movement from the farmstead to the condo has been so quick and abrupt that we suffer a permanent nostalgia for the former, which is forever just beyond the reach of experience but never out of sense-memory. This is why W.O. Mitchell, for example, was a public personality in his day, or why Stuart McLean is one today. Faux-folk, I call it. Of course, this is also true outside of the Commonwealth context. Unlike Japanese literature of the late modern period, for example, there are few skyscrapers, streetcars and nightclubs in Canadian literature, only barnyards and, more recently, bistros.

JB: That's a very interesting idea—and I think particularly inter-esting in the way you explain the general shifts you're seeing in Canadian literature as functions of its places and settings. That's an old tradition identified most prominently with the thematic critics of the late sixties and seventies—Canadian literature as the settler's response to a specific experience of a (vast, forbidding, baffling, al-ien, etc.) place and landscape. That tradition often encouraged us, I think, to see ourselves as having a literature of rural and wilderness spaces. If we're becoming more urban, I think, as your comments imply, we're also becoming more cosmopolitan: the urban spaces in our literature aren't just Toronto, Montreal, Paris and London, as of old, but lots of other Canadian cities, along with Prague, Bombay, Dar es Salaam, Port of Spain... the international list goes on and on as well. If our literature is becoming more cosmopolitan, presum-ably that has to do with three major factors: what writers are writ-ing, what readers are reading and what publishers are publishing. If

I can ask a rather complicated question, in what ways do you see these three activities affecting or influencing each other to create the current climate of literary production and consumption? Who in this system is influencing whom, and how?

GF: I honestly can't say who's influencing whom, but it's certainly clear to me that the development we've been describing is indeed a long equation of the sort you propose. However much they deny it, most writers work at what they hope they can get published, and most publishers publish what they believe they're most likely to sell—particularly when they can sell sub rights in the US, the UK and elsewhere. At least that's true for a growing number of houses. While I applaud this with one hand (yes, one hand clapping), I deplore it with the other, because this new cosmopolitanism has naturally enough led to a new parochialism as well. In the *National Post* the other day I was reading a piece by a reviewer who said he thought Canadian books that couldn't get published outside Canada were by their nature inferior. This seems to me a rather rapid return to the colonial mentality of old, for the logical extension of such thinking is, "How can stuff written here be of any value?" But I suppose the tension between internationalism of outlook and its opposite has always been one of the sources of fuel in Canadian writing—just like the tension between the rural and the urban. This is culture we're talking about, not cholesterol: it doesn't come in just two distinct varieties, the one called Good and the other Bad. The body of the nation produces both and they must always fight it out for the creative life, the energy, to continue.

JB: Do you think our notion of what belongs in a Canadian canon has changed a lot over the past decade or so?

GF: Yes. Partly because of larger forces at play, such as the rise of disciplines like gender studies, Native studies, and postcolonial studies, and the subsuming of literature into cultural studies; and partly because of smaller forces, business decisions actually—such as the shrinking of the New Canadian Library. Some or all of these factors seem to have come together to give greater importance to genre at the expense of individual works (until now, the essence of the very notion of a canon). Are there canonical works in the field of Canadian life-writing, for instance? Or is Canadian life-writing merely one genre in a canon that's now made up of genres rather than specific, permanently fixed texts? To the extent that I have a view of what the canon is from where I sit, I seem to believe that it's being renewed, refreshed, certainly expanded. Surely that's no negative development in and of itself. Which doesn't mean that poor benighted students are going to be forced to cease suffering through Grove's *Over Prairie Trails*. It means rather that they're likely to endure that pain in a different context than that in which their parents managed it. The core texts are like folk songs rather than pop songs. They survive underground and every so often they re-surface. They're studied both above ground and below, at different times, by different people.

JB: Are Canadians, by and large, adventurous readers or conservative readers?

GF: I believe that Canada, of all spots on earth, is probably the one about which it's hardest to answer such a question. Here's a place with a quarter fewer people than Burma; one very rich indeed as societies are measured, but with the tradition of humanist education, with literature as its core, lying in tatters and disrepute; where Chinese is now edging out French as the second most widely spoken language; where the people who were born here read the English-language newspapers for people who were born here and those who weren't read other English-language ones entirely; and which has only three large cities—a francophone one, another that's the craziest experimental polyphonic conurbation since Shanghai between the wars, and a third that, if it were a style of music or cuisine, would be called Asian fusion. In this situation, somehow, and I sometimes marvel at just how, a few thousand sophisticated readers of literature manage to constitute an audience in an atmosphere further distinguished by regional animosities and the national disease of constitutional hypochondria. I find this a fascinating spectacle to observe and to participate in to the extent that my limited abilities permit. I'm also interested in, and repelled by, the low rank of the writer and scholar, and the general mockery made of Can lit by most of the media. If any other country had produced Atwood, Munro, Davies and Ondaatje in one generation, citizens of that nation would be permitted to use an Author, upper case, as a guarantor of passport applications, instead of having to get a chiropractor or gym teacher to vouch for their existence. I once wrote a poem with the lines, "If this is the forest / then we must be the animals."

JB: We began by comparing the present state of publishing to the scene a generation or so ago. I wonder if we could end with some thoughts about the future—say the next ten or twenty years. What do you foresee for Canadian literature and Canadian publishing in that time? Given the general disrespect for literary endeavour that you've just mentioned, are we in danger of losing what we have?

GF: Yes, I think the danger of losing all that we've gained with such love and labour is constant and very real. Such a fragile being,

Can lit—for all its muscle tone. I worry about this a great deal but find it difficult to tell to what extent I'm witnessing simply the seasonal eclipse of one generation by the next—the natural order of things—and to what extent I'm watching the beginning of the new Dark Ages. Maybe I should have written, "If this is the new Dark Ages, / then we must be the monks." Listen to me. I sound like some old man in a brown cardigan, hanging round the barbershop because he has nothing else to do but mutter among surviving friends. Pass me that copy of *Maclean's* there, will you fella, the one with Don Messer on the cover?

JB: If you could wave a magic wand, is there anything you would like to change about the contexts and structures of Can lit production that would improve its chances of thriving for another generation or more?

GF: Long ago I took a vow never to use my magic wand for evil but only for good. I think I would have to start with getting the provinces to mandate a certain amount of Can lit be taught in schools at all levels. Everything else—publishing, bookselling—must proceed from that, I should think. Mind you, getting the provinces to agree on much of anything is not God's way.

Reading George Fetherling's Journals

Brian Busby[†]

Cravats, silk hats and walking sticks being long out of fashion, it is somewhat odd that George Fetherling is so frequently described as a "man-of-letters." The designation comes from an earlier time, a term that with age has become smudged and faded, and has lost much of its definition. Yet it serves our culture, which, like that of the Victorians, is drawn towards categorization. Similarly, Fetherling's name is frequently grouped with those of Dennis Lee, Dave Godfrey, Margaret Atwood and other figures associated with the early years of House of Anansi Press and the independent publishing movement it helped spawn. As he has often pointed out, although he was Anansi's first full-time employee, he was in the role of the kid watching the comings and goings of his elders: the most junior participant in the period characterized as the "renaissance" of Canadian literature, a decade younger than those so often described as his contemporaries. As he makes clear in *Travels by Night*, he could hardly be described as having been a guiding force at Anansi, for he was most commonly found opening the mail, answering the phone,

† Brian Busby is a literary historian and the president of the Federation of BC Writers. He is the author of *Character Parts: Who's Really Who in CanLit* (2003) and is at work on a biography of John Glassco.

filling orders and shovelling the walk. Anansi published his first book, a poetry collection, in 1968 when he was nineteen.

In his preface to *The Blue Notebook*, his 1985 collection of reviews and essays, Fetherling writes:"Since the 1960s I have laboured mostly as a cultural and political journalist, the sort known in the nineteenth century as a magazinist. The job has included spending perhaps two years with one periodical as a regular book reviewer, three years with another as film columnist, and so on, usually as a freelance but occasionally in some staff position, helping to get the publication out each month. It's not much of a living though it's not a bad life."

Here, of course, Fetherling's characteristic modesty allows for only part of the story. During those very same years he produced seven collections of poetry and other books of criticism and commentary, anticipating the long shelf of work to come, including novels, memoirs, travel narratives and volumes focusing on history, culture, the media, cinema, music and art. In Canada, the range and depth of his bibliography is perhaps surpassed by only a few figures, such as George Woodcock, of whom Fetherling wrote a biography, or Robin Skelton. Interestingly, both these writers appear frequently in Fetherling's journal, which runs to the thousands of pages.

An entry for April 28, 1981, for example, records a social evening in Vancouver:

Dinner at the Woodcocks. George: looking old now, false teeth, very Muggeridgey mouth. Inge: robust German with terrible bronchial cough and guffaw mixed as one. Jack Shadbolt: a fine leonine head, strong opinions on all sorts of subjects about which he's totally uninformed, very unpainterly and big, kids George about being on the left. Doris S.: wonderful Ontario accent and manner, straight, earnest, decent, like a middle-aged Jan Walter. Paul Wong [who] runs Bau-Xi Gallery on the coast and in Toronto. His wife: 40 year old anglo, looks younger [...] I arrive first and have an hour of literary and other chat with George in his den, not so many books as I would have imagined, the old portable manual typewriter he uses for all purposes set up on a large folding table. He says his health is fine now, he attributes his heart attack in the 60s to stress of teaching two new courses and writing three books all at once. I'd have thought that if anyone could do that [...] Cocktails then dinner in the small dining room of this very English house ($14,800 20 years ago, now because of the land worth $200,000, according to "estate agents") filled with objects from travels [...] Topics from George then and after dinner range from art patronage in 15th-century Germany to the iconography of the wild roses on Hornby Island as opposed to that of those on the mainland, all this without the slightest trace of arrogance or brashness or even awareness of what it is he's doing [...] Woodcocks have a clawless cat named Alfie that looks like Groucho Marx and that they took in from the pound years ago when it appeared the creature would be killed. Inge and I feed the raccoons on the back porch: a nightly ritual.

As for Skelton, an entry from May 1989 reads:

J and I celebrate our sixth anniversary a week late. Last year we ran into Robin Skelton and dragged him along to our anniversary dinner (telling him that this seemed only fair, seeing that he had been excluded from the honeymoon). This year we find ourselves invited to a party for him at Arlene Lampert's. The hostess [and] everyone in fine form, [and] Robin looking dazed as usual. I asked him what books he has coming out or in the works and he withdrew a neatly numbered list of 20 titles. Running me through it, he cursed that he had forgotten one. Later still, another stray occurred to him. We had to leave before the count reached 23.

Later still, in February 1991, there is a memorable description of the Skelton residence in Victoria:

> We get away on an early ferry, and the Skeltons meet us at the depot at the other end, Sylvia looking patient, competent and satisfied, and Robin, in his black felt Robert Graves hat, looking almost as befuddled as he is. J can only guess how the neighbours in Oak Bay must view the Skelton ménage, full of poets, witches, and other visitors, including on-and-off-again children. The house is huge (there are still bells for ringing the servants) and stuffed with books and pictures and carvings and junk and all of it absolutely filthy [...] In the back garden is a circle of charred stones, indicating where ceremonies are conducted.

To date, this journal has not been published except for brief excerpts in a slim private-press book entitled *Notes from a Journal, 1978–1980*. It was produced in 1987 by a Toronto artist, George Walker, who illustrated it with his wood engravings and printed it by hand in a signed and numbered edition of 126 copies, giving a tiny number of readers a brief, teasing look at what is in effect Fetherling's longest work. Given his prolificacy and ease with the written word, it shouldn't be a surprise that Fetherling is a meticulous journal-keeper, though the exact purpose and nature of the journal have changed over the years, as have the physical journals in which he writes, usually in longhand, and at certain periods much more legibly than at others. The earliest surviving journal (others, says Fetherling, have been lost along the way through various moves and others traumas) is dated 1975 and begins with an entry about Robert Fulford ("at home with the ague") and soon moves on to accounts of meetings with other figures in Canadian writing, as with this poignant entry from February:

> Call Gwen MacEwen on an impulse and am invited to

her place for coffee, her Greek husband being away (ominously) in Montreal [...] She's grotesquely puffed up and talking nonsense. Illustrating her technique of pain control, she spends the whole evening passing her hands slowly through a lighted candle till her hands are black from carbon up to her wrists. Also there is a fellow Gwen introduces as a psychic, who insists I am a student and from the West. Filled with sadness after seeing Gwen, I trudge these old neighbourhoods in the rain.

This 1975 journal is written on leaves torn from an appointment book and held together by a metal clip, while the next volume in the sequence consists of hundreds of cerlox-bound pages, most typewritten on the reverse of old CBC scripts and publicity releases. One more recent volume resembles a religious tract; it has been bound in black boards with the title *War News* stamped in gold on the front. Some of the journals have a professional appearance, being written in the lovely Moleskine notebooks from Britain favoured by Bruce Chatwin and others or in highly tactile Clairefontaine notebooks from France. One of the journals is actually bound in full calf, with raised bands. Many others, however, seem to make use of whatever stationery was nearest to hand, such as school exercise books evidently grabbed during travels but used only much later. For example, one journal is written in an exam book from the South Pacific and another, on the cheapest imaginable paper, appears to have begun life as a student's scribbler in—judging from the alphabet of the cover text—Burma.

Until very recent times it would have been socially acceptable to say that Fetherling's journal was born out of disability. He began the document as a part of speech therapy, in which journal-keeping is recommended practice. The initial purpose was to provide a record of each day's conversations in order to discern patterns and particular situations or individuals or combinations of sounds associated with stuttering. Reading these early entries, which at times record his handicap in agonizing detail, one quickly becomes aware of what will be the enduring value of these journals: the author's thirty years of running commentary on the personalities and vicissitudes of Canadian literature. In his daily struggles to communicate, to claim a place and earn a living, Fetherling encounters people on the fringes and within the vortex of the literary world. What is more, his interests and assignments as a sometime cultural journalist bring him into contact with politicians, entrepreneurs, philosophers, broadcasters, actors and artists: a cross-section of the most conspicuous figures of our time. "Lunch today with Conrad Black," a page from 1980 begins. The following year, one finds this:

> Dinner tonight with Gore Vidal, who seemed to us as charming and cordial as ever he gets with outsiders (look what he writes about even his few old friends like Tennessee Williams). P reports that he flashed a curious look for an instant on the first occasion my speech faltered but that he took in the situation in a mini-second. "He's a gentleman from the inside out" was her comment. Generally the session went very well: I (falteringly) talked ideas while P charmed it out. When he's truly amused (and not always at his own remarks) a marvellous intelligent and feminine smile engulfs the lower part of his face […] He's well informed about Canada, which was pleasant for a change. When he spoke of being from a region ancestrally where many people are descended from Roman legionnaires, I could see the connexion at once. His head would look perfect on a coin, said P.

From its clinical beginnings, in fact, Fetherling's journal has evolved, shifting in form and content to serve its creator. It has provided support as a writer's notebook, an *aide mémoire* and a repository of quotations, observations and thoughts. A significant portion could be excised and published as a rather humorous dream diary, and two pamphlets, one sexual, the other political, could be made from the graffiti recorded on daily walks. First and foremost, however, the journal is a record of one writer's experiences during the healthiest and most turbulent period in Canadian letters. It provides a glimpse into the process of literary creation, from the initial spark, through the lengthy writing process, to publication and critical reception but not, tellingly, to the receipt of royalty cheques.

Among its pages can be found details of days sacrificed to "bread work," unpaid labour and unrealized projects. For the inquisitive, the journal offers something of a sketch of the self-discipline and politics involved in earning a living as a writer, an interest that Fetherling shares with many of us. In a 1980 entry, he admits:

> My main interest in reading biography and the more journalistic sort of literary studies has been to learn about the minutiae of public careers. I have always been fascinated to learn of other people's work habits: what hours they wrote, how they conducted their business, where exactly they fitted in on the stages of their time. I believe this interest has been partly aimed at locating habits worthy of emulation (or theft). But there's also a more pressing need: to make me rationalize, or conjure up, as the case may be, where I might stand or don't stand in regard to public-ness. All things considered an appalling habit.

As the years pass, the journal born in therapy takes on a different curative role. It becomes a device through which the author reflects on professional grievances and wrongs, a dialogue with the self through which lessons are learned and wounds are healed.

Fetherling's early writing coincided with a great qualitative change in Canada's literature, yet for many years he has struggled for acceptance. As he writes in *Travels by Night*, he is self-taught. Although he has taught at the university level, his absence of formal education has limited employment prospects. His sole degree is an honorary Doctor of Letters from St. Mary's University in Halifax. "From the Jesuits, even though I am not a Roman Catholic," he likes to joke. "What this proves is that to appreciate my beauty, you must be slightly outside the mainstream." His long battle for recognition has, on occasion, led to temporary resignation. In a 1998 entry he writes: "All I have ever wanted to be, for the past 30 years, was a fellow Canadian writer. After the same thirty years of being told that I do not qualify, I am finally losing the ambition, and have nothing to replace it." In another entry he records his desire to flee "the niggling, in-fighting and bitterness of the literary world with its destroyed personalities." Yet he is forever drawn to the writing life, a chosen vocation which has provided his food, clothing and shelter since he was a young teenager.

> Growing older and reading I realize what others must always have known: that the bright moments in any life, whether public recognition or personal triumph, must inevitably fall amid the usual long run of tedium and drudgery. The proper approach to this reality seems to be an acceptance of it, an understanding that the predictable workaday existence is what makes possible the sudden and usually quite unpredictable relief. Reputation often consists of how one manages other people's recognition of such things. All the more reason not to do so.

At one point, I asked Fetherling whether he has been aware of his journal as a part of a broader tradition of such works, both here and abroad. He replied this way:

> After enough time has elapsed, many journals of course acquire interest as social history. Some are even written with that in mind (Cecil Beaton's, for example). I believe I'm correct in saying that while writers often have published their diaries during their lifetimes, these have tended to be works of social observation. Arnold Bennett's, for instance.

As far as I know, the vogue for living writers to publish more serious journals comes from Gide.

Journals as lit? Well, unlike some of the more self-conscious diary writers, most habitual diary readers don't consider such journals literature—"any more than I think statues are sculpture," my artist friend Vera Frenkel once said to me. The comparison with statuary seems especially apt in the case of those endless formal diaries that certain public figures have kept as strictly as a religious observance for the purpose of ensuring their posthumous fame: the diaries of people such as Beaton and Harold Nicolson or, from a different mob, the Labour politician Richard Crossman. Vera went on to say: "Gossip and self-revelation—interchangeable, perhaps—are endlessly intriguing, and for me, can appear in fairly rough-and-ready form without losing any interest." Most of us feel the same, I'd bet.

Fetherling's journal demonstrates, better than any biography or memoir, the experience of being a Canadian writer during the past three decades. It runs counter to the fanciful but still prevalent image of the writer as an independent spirit blessed with lavish advances and abundant royalties. Rather, it is vivid evidence of a man (of letters) working under numerous pressures, not the least of which being those he places on his own self.

Voice Mail
or
Not To Be Opened 'Til My Death

JENNIFER TOEWS[†]

The world is too much with us
we have given our hearts away
says the man taking notes at the party
Rites of Alienation

George Fetherling and I have never met, yet I feel that I know him. We have, however, chatted by email, telephone and fax, though I would say that I feel I know him best through his personal papers. His annual gifts of such material to the Thomas Fisher Rare Book Library at the University of Toronto reflect aspects of his life and work that he wishes to be remembered, such as the fact that his paternal grandfather had the unusual habit of collecting murder weapons, a passion that may well have influenced Fetherling to write *The Book of Assassins* in 2001. Like many writers, he is a natural archivist, meticulously organizing and documenting evidence of his life and writing. His papers reflect a sense of meditative, thoughtful order—they don't reek of cigarettes, perfume or mould, and they aren't crumpled, stained or ragged. Their condition suggests careful, almost reverent treatment, as though he knew that one

---

[†] Jennifer Toews is a manuscript librarian at the Thomas Fisher Rare Book Library, University of Toronto.

day he would give them to the library for safekeeping. The Fisher Library at the University of Toronto, which collects the papers of Gwendolyn MacEwen, Dennis Lee, Margaret Atwood, Leonard Cohen and David Solway, to name just a few of its more than sixty Canadian literature manuscript collections, is open to all interested researchers.

George maintains an active interest in this material, and I'll receive an email from him from time to time, asking for confirmation of some elusive detail that can only be found in his papers:

GF: [C]ould you bear to wallow in previous donations for a bit of information? You should have there my appointment book for 1990. Can you figure out what days I was in Chongqing in China during either May or June? (Chongqing followed Beijing but came before Shanghai if that helps.)

GF: Dear Jennifer: I just thought of something. The library, I think, would have my cancelled passport for 1990. The immigration stamps would give you the opening and closing dates of the China trip. With that info, finding the Chongqing dates in the appointment book will be *much* easier. Thanks. George

JT: Hi George, I'm still looking for your passport and appointment book, but I have come across a listing for Box 102, "Restricted Diaries." Is this what you are referring to? The note you sent us with them states "Not to be opened until my death." They are dated 1987–96 and are tied and sealed. Thanks. Jennifer

GF: Dear J: Hmmm, I think those are daily appointment books, Brownline leatherette-bound things, about 3 x 5 inches. If so, that would be where I made note of where I had to be on a particular day—i.e., this is where the answer to the Chongqing question would lie. So go ahead and look there. The passport, if you have it, would help narrow down the search to just a few days. Thanks. G

JT: Hi, George: Okay, I have copied below your location notes for May 11–20, 1990:

> May 11—Beijing
> May 12—Beijing—free day
> May 13—Beijing—Chongqing "flite"
> May 14—Chongqing
> May 15—Chongqing
> May 16—river, boat
> May 17—river, boat, flight to Wuhan
> May 18—Wuhan
> May 19—Wuhan to Shanghai
> May 20—Shanghai

GF: That was quite a trip, that one. The Soviet Union was disintegrating quickly, and I left on the Trans-Siberian train via Inner Mongolia, a journey of almost a week, I believe. When I got there, the Chinese thought I was a spy, because, after they first refused me a visa, I'd asked Joe Clark to intercede. "How does this nobody know his foreign affairs minister?" they must have said to themselves. Merry hijinx. Yes, you can reseal those appointment books in their lead coffin. Thanks. And yes please let me know if you turn up any errant journals.

George's papers reflect his adventurous, nomadic life. *Running Away to Sea: Round the World on a Tramp Freighter* documents his extensive voyage travelling as a passenger on a cargo ship. Following the publication of this work, he donated chapters of the book, which were mailed to his assistant as individual letters from Brazil, Argentina, the Falkland Islands, Chile and elsewhere. They are innovative in form, and remind the reader of an older genre, the *dispatch*.

In the course of working with his papers over the past few years, I've learned how George chooses his subjects for their interest and impact, mixing the political with the everyday: "Dead street late at night / even the homeless gone home / a blind man's cane protruding from the garbage" (*Rites of Alienation*, 5) or "Conscience and indigestion / danger increases as the seasons change / Utopia made her claustrophobic" (*Rites of Alienation*, 13).

A notable Toronto antiquarian bookseller has described George to me as a "writer's writer." I've read the documentation concerning such matters as George's decisions to purchase *Canadian Notes and Queries* to keep it alive until another publisher could be found or donate his cabin on Quesnel Lake in the Cariboo district of BC as a retreat for writers. Such acts show how deeply he cares about Canada and its writers.

Panning For Gold

Rhonda Batchelor[†]

I believe I first met George Fetherling in Victoria in either 1990 or 1991. He and his (then) wife Janet Inksetter were visiting Robin and Sylvia Skelton. It seems to me that Janet was possibly engaged in offering some professional book-dealer's advice to the Skeltons with regard to their impressive but increasingly cumbersome library. Their visit must have included a Monday night stopover, for they attended one of the regular readings held at the Hawthorne Bookshop. In 1990, Robin and Sylvia, along with my husband, Charles Lillard, and a handful of other possibly misguided souls, had founded the Hawthorne Society of Arts and Letters. This rather grand name concealed a humble, extremely non-profit organization primarily dedicated to promoting the literary arts in Greater Victoria. Part of its mandate included the hosting of a monthly poetry reading at Hawthorne Books, a shop operated by Horst Martin, with me its sole employee.

I don't recall who was reading the night that George and Janet were in attendance, but I do remember that six of us (the Fetherlings, Skeltons and Lillards) piled into Sylvia's car, aka the Floating

[†] Rhonda Batchelor is a poet and small-press publisher and one of the editors of *Malahat Review*.

Living Room, and adjourned to Christie's Carriage House, a pub much loved by Robin and Charles, especially after mornings at the flea market. I ended up sitting beside Janet in the noisy pub and, since we were both booksellers and she was charming, knowledgeable and amusing, I was happy to more or less talk exclusively with her that evening.

But George had already made a most favourable impression. Tall and slender, with long fingers and finely boned hands, he was dressed elegantly (by West Coast standards). His voice was modulated and careful; I was unaware, during our first meeting, that he suffered from a speech impediment—it simply wasn't evident to me. I sensed he was an essentially shy man who nevertheless contributed easily to the conversation whirling round him. He asked pointed questions and listened with a journalist's ear. His repertoire of anecdotes, one sensed, was probably bottomless, but he would never offer one up unless it directly augmented the topic on the table.

George and Charles had never met before, but they clicked immediately. I think I was a bit surprised at this, for my husband was not one to open up to strangers or to show much curiosity towards them. It often took several encounters, and, even then, unless those encounters proved sufficiently rewarding intellectually, Charles simply couldn't be bothered to make much of an effort. This wasn't unkindness; it was just a case of his often being preoccupied. Of course, George's reputation had preceded him, as Charles's had; the two had much in common.

Charles was born in California in 1944 and raised in southeastern Alaska, and had come to Canada in the early 1960s. Summers spent clearing streams in remote wilderness areas of British Columbia financed his formal studies at UBC, where he earned a master's degree in creative writing. More importantly, they served as a spawning ground for his poetry and his vision of the Pacific Northwest. Except for sporadic stints of teaching, Charles worked outside the academy, earning a meagre living as a freelance writer while pursuing historical research and eventually writing about thirty-five books. He cared passionately about the state of reviewing in this country and did what he could to promote the work of other writers. When local papers cut their allotted review space, he financed his own fortnightly review sheet, distributed free of charge in Victoria bookshops. But primarily he considered himself a poet, and rightly so.

George was the younger by five years and had spent most of his life in Toronto where poetry, politics and publishing (in no particular order) began to work on him—as he worked on them. His association with Dave Godfrey, Dennis Lee and Anansi and other presses introduced him to a plethora of characters who shared nothing if not a zestful energy characteristic of the 1960s and 1970s. Before long, George was leading the pack, not only in the number of publications, but in the range of his endeavours, which grew to include visual art as well.

It must have been at Christie's pub or in correspondence thereafter that Charles invited George to put together a "checklist" of his own major publications to date. Reference West, the press we had founded to publish chapbooks for the Hawthorne Society, had already printed two such bibliographies by Skelton and George Woodcock. In the introduction to the one George compiled, which we published as a chapbook in 1991 called *Catalogus* in an edition of 250 copies, he is characteristically humble:

> Some might think it egotistical to accept an invitation to put together a checklist such as this. I suspected just the opposite—that confronting the work one now automatically disowns would be an act of the severest self-criticism, such as the Red Guards during the Cultural Revolution in China might have envied and admired. I was correct. Looking at this inventory, I can't escape the conclusion that I published almost nothing worth publishing until 1985 and that

progress since then has been spotty at best. Chastened but
refreshed, humiliated but cleansed, I push on.

Chastened or not, Fetherling was able to list seventy-seven entries
(excluding all periodical appearances) covering the years 1968 to
1990. That's an average of 3.5 book and chapbook publications per
year in areas as diverse as poetry, travel writing, biography, cultural
history, film, music and criticism.

In 1992, George was again invited to publish under the Reference West imprint, this time as a poet. I was particularly pleased to
have the opportunity to publish someone who had been part of
an anthology that had greatly influenced my own early aspirations.
Storm Warning: The New Canadian Poets, edited by Al Purdy, had appeared in 1971 when I was a Grade 12 student in Ontario, a brave
collection that opened my eyes to the possibility of being a real
poet even if young, even if Canadian. I had no idea, back then, that
I would one day count as friends not only the book's editor but
also several of the writers represented, including Fetherling, Patrick
Lane, bill bissett, David McFadden and David Zieroth. The chapbook George contributed to the Hawthorne series was entitled
Chinese Anthology and was dedicated "For Sharon Thesen in admiration." Of course the combination launch and reading required
George's presence and was thus timed to correspond with his next
visit (solo this time) to Victoria. I remember that P.K. Page was in
the front row, smiling to herself throughout his reading. We were
all smiling; the poems were wonderful, inspired in part by George's
travels in China. Here is one stanza from the book's final poem,
"Dreaming in the Pluperfect":

Events befall as usual. You cannot prevent them
from doing so. In the end, our dreams will be the only proof
that we were here, the warranty of efficient progress and
honest feeling. Newton's second law: objects in motion

tend to remain in motion if they have any say in the matter.
In the end, finally, it becomes a question of making salvation
look graceful.

George stayed at our home during that visit. Once again I was
struck by the easy communication between George and Charles,
a camaraderie based on mutual respect. I think it was during that
stay (or one the next year) that George sat in our living room and
read to us from the manuscript of *Travels by Night*, his "memoir
of the sixties." Charles and I were spellbound as George read the
first chapter in its entirety. Until that evening, we hadn't known
anything of his background or of his fairly horrendous childhood.
It was sobering to say the least. We were even more in awe of his
accomplishments, given the daunting circumstances he'd had to
overcome.

George Fetherling has an international reputation as a talented
and prolific writer, yet his personal life has always remained just
that. The shyness I sensed at our first meeting may or may not be
more than a general guardedness—a policy of holding his cards
close to his chest. But George is a generous individual too. Not
unlike Robin Skelton or George Woodcock, he is a man who can
always find time to help aspiring writers or struggling publishers,
often with a well-timed article that will give them some much-
needed press.

Following my husband's death from cancer in 1997, a number
of tributes poured in, from formal recognition from the British
Columbia legislature to the hundreds of personal notes I received
from friends and acquaintances. I was touched by the high esteem
in which his memory was held. There were also notices in several
publications ranging from the local and Vancouver papers to historical journals and literary magazines. But it was an obituary written
by George for the Lives Lived column of the *Globe and Mail*, some

four months after Charles's death, that seemed to get to the essence of what his life had been all about.

It chronicled the usual facts: where he'd lived, his education, his various occupations and publications. It also noted the range of his interests and the dichotomy of a man often (mis)labelled a "logger poet" being, in fact, an environmentalist. He was, George could see, "not an armchair person who dreamed of adventure but rather an outdoors person with a deep knowledge of books and culture. His physical appearance and manner—burly, rough-and-tumble, somewhat hard-living and sometimes brusque while kindly—disguised his deep love of the lamp." Yet the most startling and satisfying section of this tribute was in the final paragraph:

> When Charles was diagnosed with cancer, I manufactured occasions to check in with him by telephone. (He had a magnificent telephone voice, and could easily have been a professional broadcaster if he had wished.) In one conversation I casually mentioned that I had just received my Free Miner's certificate in BC. A few months later, a parcel arrived from Charles. It was his old gold pan, dented from long use and nicely oxidized. There was no note. The gesture was the note. Charles was handing over a symbol of himself.

And he was. As I interpret it, especially in relation to both of these remarkable men, it represents day-by-day working: a loving process in itself but one which, if done long enough and carefully enough, paying attention to the shiny details, can bring untold reward. Charles knew that George of all people would understand.

Selected Bibliography

United States of Heaven. Toronto: Anansi, 1968. Poetry.

My Experience in the War. Toronto: Weed/Flower Press, 1970. Poetry.

Our Man in Utopia. Toronto: Macmillan, 1971. Poetry.

Café Terminus. Toronto: Missing Link Press, 1973. Poetry.

Eleven Early Poems. Toronto: Weed/Flower Press, 1973. Poetry.

Achilles' Navel. Erin, Ontario: Press Porcépic, 1974. Poetry.

The Five Lives of Ben Hecht. Toronto: Lester & Orpen, 1977. New York: New York Zoetrope, 1980. Cinema.

Gold Diggers of 1929. Toronto: Macmillan, 1979, 1986 (revised edition). Toronto: John Wiley, 2004.

A George Woodcock Reader (editor). Ottawa: Deneau & Greenburg, 1980.

Subroutines. Toronto: League of Canadian Poets, 1981. Poetry.

The Blue Notebook: Reports on Canadian Culture. Oakville: Mosaic Press, 1985. Kingston: Quarry Press, 1991. Toronto: Subway Books, 1995. Essays.

Carl Sandburg at the Movies: A Poet in the Silent Era 1920–1927 (editor, with Dale Fetherling). Metuchen, New Jersey: Scarecrow Press, 1985. Cinema.

Variorum: New Poems and Old, 1965–1985. Toronto: Hounslow Press, 1985. Kingston: Quarry Press, 1991. Toronto: Subway Books, 1998.

Dead Man's Shoes. Toronto: Letters, 1986. Poetry.

Four Corners. Toronto: jwcurry, 1986. Poetry.

Moving Towards the Vertical Horizon. Toronto: Subway Books, 1986. Poetry.

Documents in Canadian Art (editor). Peterborough: Broadview Press, 1987.

Notes from a Journal 1978–1980. Toronto: Columbus Street Press, 1987.

The Broadview Book of Canadian Anecdotes (editor). Peterborough: Broadview Press, 1988.

The Crowded Darkness. Kingston: Quarry Press, 1988. Toronto: Subway Books, 1999. Essays.

Documents in Canadian Film (editor). Peterborough: Broadview Press, 1988.

The Gold Crusades: A Social History of Gold Rushes, 1849–1929. Toronto: Macmillan, 1988. Toronto: University of Toronto Press, 1997 (revised edition).

Rites of Alienation. Kingston: Quarry Press, 1988. Toronto: Subway Books, 1990. Poetry.

Best Canadian Essays 1989 (editor). Saskatoon: Fifth House Publishers, 1989.

Memorandum for the File. Toronto: Roger Burford Mason, 1989. Poetry.

Best Canadian Essays 1990 (editor). Saskatoon: Fifth House Publishers, 1990.

The Rise of the Canadian Newspaper. Toronto: Oxford University Press, 1990. History.

Catalogus. Victoria: Reference West, 1991. Bibliography.

The Dreams of Ancient Peoples. Toronto: ECW Press, 1991. Poetry.

Some Day Soon: Essays on Canadian Songwriters. Kingston: Quarry Press, 1991.

Year of the Horse: A Journey through Russia & China. Toronto: Stoddart Publishing, 1991.

Chinese Anthology. Victoria: Reference West, 1992. Poetry.

A Little Bit of Thunder. Toronto: Stoddart, 1993. History.

Travels by Night: A Memoir of the Sixties. Toronto: Lester, 1994. Toronto: McArthur, 2000.

Selected Poems. Vancouver: Arsenal Pulp Press, 1994. Vancouver: Subway Books, 2005.

Letters Outward. Toronto: Sintax Press, 1995. Poetry.

The Other China: Journeys Around Taiwan. Vancouver: Arsenal Pulp Press, 1995. Toronto: Subway Books, 2000.

Way Down Deep in the Belly of the Beast: A Memoir of the Seventies. Toronto: Lester, 1996. Toronto: McArthur, 2000.

The File on Arthur Moss. Toronto: Lester, 1998. Toronto: Subway Books, 2000. Novel.

The Gentle Anarchist: A Life of George Woodcock. Vancouver: Douglas & McIntyre, 1998. Seattle: University of Washington Press, 1998. Vancouver: Subway Books, 2003.

Running Away to Sea: Round the World on a Tramp Freighter. Toronto: McClelland and Stewart, 1998.

Madagascar: Poems & Translations. Windsor: Black Moss Press, 1999.

A Biographical Dictionary of the World's Assassins. Toronto: Random House, 2001. London: Robert Hale, 2002. Tokyo: Harashobo, 2003. Prague: Oldag, 2004. (Also published as *The Book of Assassins.* New York: John Wiley, 2002. Toronto: Vintage, 2005.)

The Vintage Book of Canadian Memoirs (editor). Toronto: Random House, 2001.

Jive Talk: George Fetherling in Interviews & Documents (edited by Joe Blades). Fredericton: Broken Jaw Press, 2001.

Three Pagodas Pass: A Roundabout Journey to Burma. Vancouver: Subway Books, 2002. Bangkok: Asia Books, 2003.

Singer, An Elegy. Vancouver: Anvil Press, 2004. Poetry.

One Russia Two Chinas. Vancouver: Beach Holme Publishing, 2004.

Jericho. Toronto: Random House, 2005. Novel.

Tales of Two Cities. Vancouver: Subway Books, 2006. Novella and stories.

604 958-1349